ACKNOWLEDGEMENTS

The creation of this book would not have been possible without the help of many people. I was supported by a group of talented individuals through the entire process of conceiving the idea, conducting market research, writing and editing the manuscript, designing the cover and formatting the book's layout, printing, marketing and now collecting feedback and communicating with small business owners.

Special thanks to my wife Dina who supported and inspired me during many months of writing this book as well as provided editorial and marketing advice.

I greatly appreciate the assistance of Peter Stephan who was invaluable in marketing this book to make sure that it reaches its target audience – you, the small business owner. My appreciation also extends to lenders across the United States who gave me their advice and input, which made this book a priceless source of financial knowledge for millions of entrepreneurs.

Finally, I would like to thank those business men and women who were generous with their time to review this book and offer their feedback. I also want to thank you for purchasing this book and giving me a chance to help you with your loan financing needs.

Warm Regards,

D. Neil Berdiev

NOTICE TO READERS

All rights reserved. The information, data, artwork, text, text structure, pictures, and other intellectual property, including the selection and arrangement thereof, are protected by copyright and other intellectual property laws. You may not decompile, disassemble, rent, lease, loan, sublicense, or create derivative works from this publication. You may not copy, modify, reproduce, republish, distribute, transmit, or use this work for commercial or other purposes, unless you obtain a written permission from D. Neil Berdiev or his authorized officer(s). Printers (Publishers) On Demand may not be Mr. Berdiev's authorized officers. For details on how to obtain the permission, you may contact Mr. Berdiev by email at neil@loanfinancingguide.com (please write "permission requested" in the subject field). Please note that the contact information may change from time to time. It is your responsibility to ensure that a person or an entity giving you an authorization is indeed authorized by the author to act on his behalf.

This book is not intended to be and is not legal, accounting, or other professional advice or service. It is limited to the field of loan financing. For questions related to legal, accounting, or other professional issues, please seek the help of qualified professionals in those fields. Not every loan officer or his or her employer will agree with all the information provided in this book. The majority of examples presented in this book are real life companies; however, names and sometimes industries of those small businesses were changed to protect the identities of businesses and their owners. The author's knowledge extends to the overall knowledge of the lending industry. However, because of the possibilities of human and mechanical error, as well as unforeseen factors beyond the control of D. Neil Berdiev, his business partners, associates, or affiliates, Mr. Berdiev makes no representations or warranties of any kind in connection with this information. Please understand that business landscape, practices, culture, environment, and regulations are constantly changing, and these materials may not be complete or accurate as of the date you receive or review them. Every effort was made to keep this book as current as possible. However, the author, his associates, business partners, and affiliates make no representations or warranties regarding the outcome and the results to which the use of this book is put and are not assuming any liability for any claims, losses, damages arising from use or misuse of this book, whether monetary or non-monetary.

Loan Financing Guide for Small Business Owners

D. Neil Berdiev

© 2005 D. Neil Berdiev

All rights reserved.

No part of this book may be used or reproduced in any manner without written permission except for brief quotations used in reviews and critiques.

Printed in the United States of America.

Published by
Small Business Empowerment Publishing
Boston, MA
www.loanfinancingguide.com

ISBN 0-9774117-0-2
EAN 978-0-9774117-0-2
First Edition 2006

Library of Congress Cataloging-in-Publication Data

Berdiev, Neil.
 Loan financing guide for small business owners / by Neil Berdiev.-- 1st ed.
   p. cm.
 ISBN-13: 978-0-9774117-0-2 (alk. paper)
 ISBN-10: 0-9774117-0-2
 1. Small business--Finance--Handbooks, manuals, etc. 2. Small business--United States--Finance. I. Title.
 HG4027.7.B478 2006
 658.15'224--dc22
                    2005032780

I have enjoyed a rewarding career as a banker. What made it particularly memorable is an opportunity to work with small businesses and serve their financing needs. Over the last five years alone, I have personally participated in the analysis and approval of more than $50 million in loan requests to small businesses. Furthermore, I worked for very large as well as small community banks, experiencing first hand how they fulfill the financing needs of small enterprises. Unfortunately, I saw again and again small business loan requests denied because the owners of those companies did not know how to present their requests in the best possible light.

I love what I do, I do it well, and I created this book to help you get the loans your business needs.

D. Neil Berdiev

CONTENTS

INTRODUCTION 1

BEFORE PREPARING A LOAN REQUEST 5
    CHAPTER 1 - SIMPLY DEBT: CONS AND PROS 7
    CHAPTER 2 – TRANSLATING YOUR BUSINESS GOALS INTO
        DEBT FINANCING TERMS 11
    CHAPTER 3 – THE IMPORTANCE OF KNOWING HOW MUCH,
        WHY, AND HOW 15
    CHAPTER 4 - HOW MUCH IS TOO MUCH? 19
    CHAPTER 5 - DO YOU NEED A LOAN PROPOSAL? 25
    CHAPTER 6 – A QUICK OVERVIEW OF FINANCIAL CONCEPTS THAT ARE
        USEFUL IN APPLYING FOR LOANS 29
    CHAPTER 7 – LENDING TERMINOLOGY AND CONCEPTS FOR SMALL
        BUSINESS OWNERS 35

PREPARING A LOAN REQUEST (CASH FLOW FACTORS) 45
    CHAPTER 8 - ANALYZING YOUR HISTORICAL FINANCIAL PERFORMANCE
        AND STAYING ONE STEP AHEAD OF LENDERS 47
    CHAPTER 9 - EVALUATING YOUR CASH FLOW BASED ON HISTORICAL
        VERSUS PROJECTED FINANCIAL STATEMENTS 53
    CHAPTER 10 – DETERMINING YOUR FINANCING NEEDS: HOW MUCH YOU
        NEED VERSUS HOW MUCH YOU CAN AFFORD 57
    CHAPTER 11 – DOES YOUR FINANCING REQUEST MAKE SENSE? 63

PREPARING A LOAN REQUEST (NON-CASH FLOW FACTORS) 67
    CHAPTER 12 – COLLATERAL 69
    CHAPTER 13 - PERSONAL GUARANTEE 73
    CHAPTER 14 – PERSONAL CREDIT HISTORY 77
    CHAPTER 15 – QUALITY OF YOUR MANAGEMENT TEAM 81
    CHAPTER 16 – BUSINESS CREDIT HISTORY 83
    CHAPTER 17 – THE FIVE CS OF CREDIT AND WHY YOU NEED TO
        KNOW THEM 85

PUTTING ALL THE INFORMATION TOGETHER 89
    CHAPTER 18 – ORGANIZING YOUR INFORMATION 91
    CHAPTER 19 – MOCK INTERVIEWS AND PREPARATION FOR MEETINGS
        WITH LENDERS 95

KNOW YOUR LENDER **99**

    CHAPTER 20 – THE BANKING ENVIRONMENT AND HOW IT
        BENEFITS YOU 101
    CHAPTER 21 – WHAT LENDERS EXPECT 103
    CHAPTER 22 – LENDER'S PET PEEVES: SITUATIONS TO AVOID 105
    CHAPTER 23 – HELP LENDERS UNDERSTAND YOUR INDUSTRY AND
        MAKE THEM MORE COMFORTABLE WITH YOUR LOAN REQUEST .. 109
    CHAPTER 24 – LENDERS' PERSONALITIES 113
    CHAPTER 25 – HOW LENDERS REVIEW YOUR LOAN REQUEST AND
        WHAT IT MEANS TO YOU 117

FINDING A LENDER **121**

    CHAPTER 26 – ASSESSING YOUR CHANCES OF GETTING A LOAN 123
    CHAPTER 27 – CHOICE OF LENDERS AND CREDIT PRODUCTS 129
    CHAPTER 28 – LOANS FROM RELATIVES, FRIENDS, AND OTHER
        PRIVATE INDIVIDUALS 133
    CHAPTER 29 – PRE-INTERVIEWS OF LENDERS 139
    CHAPTER 30 – CHOOSING AND APPLYING 143

MORE USEFUL INFORMATION **147**

    CHAPTER 31 – BEING HONEST WITH LENDERS IN GOOD TIMES AND
        IN BAD TIMES: PROS AND CONS 149
    CHAPTER 32 – MANAGING YOUR SATISFACTION WITH LENDERS 153
    CHAPTER 33 – NEGOTIATING PRICING 155
    CHAPTER 34 – OTHER VALUABLE POINTS 157

APPENDICES **161**

    APPENDIX 1 - CONVERTING YOUR BUSINESS AND PERSONAL GOALS INTO
        THE LANGUAGE LENDERS WILL UNDERSTAND AND APPRECIATE 163
    APPENDIX 2 - A POSSIBLE INCOME STATEMENT FORMAT 169
    APPENDIX 3 - STATEMENT OF CASH FLOWS 171
    APPENDIX 4 - HISTORICAL INCOME STATEMENT OF RESTAURANT X 173
        HISTORICAL BALANCE SHEET OF RESTAURANT X 174
    APPENDIX 5 - AN APPROACH TO ESTIMATING YOUR BUSINESS' ABILITY
        TO MAKE LOAN PAYMENTS 175

INTRODUCTION

This book was created for you, the small business owner, to teach you everything about securing loans: from choosing loans as a possible financing source for your company, to applying for a loan, to improving your chances of being approved for a loan, to learning everything you need to know about the loan approval process, to staying in control of the loan application process. As an added bonus, this book will help you determine when loans are not an appropriate source of financing, and provide you with inside knowledge on loan officers' expectations, preferences, and pet peeves. This book is a simple, practical, and effective step-by-step guide to achieving your financing goals in the least amount of time.

Many business owners ask why it is important to know how bankers and other lenders think, operate, and make loan decisions. The answer is simple – each bit of knowledge improves your chances of securing the financing your business seeks and brings your company a step closer to becoming more successful than its competition. Let me ask you a question. Would you open an upscale restaurant in a neighborhood that was experiencing an increase in crime? Would you begin developing a software program if several of your competitors were in the process of developing a similar product and were likely to complete it before you did? I hope your answer is either "no" or at least "it depends". In either case, you conduct the necessary research and adjust your actions appropriately. Another example is a sports team that not only trains, but also studies its competitors' game, and even non-competitors, to learn how to become better. So why would you want to seek debt financing (also known as loans), if you do not know exactly what you are going up against and what the rules of the game are?

To be successful in the financing game, you must learn how to present your request in the most appealing way. This knowledge will ensure that you will not waste your time and money pursuing financing you do not have a chance of obtaining, or financing that is not appropriate for your goals. This book will help you focus on what is attainable. Moreover, this knowledge will help you secure the terms, conditions, and pricing that is most advantageous to your company under given circumstances.

Did you know that there are 25 million businesses in the United States, 71% of which have no employees (a one-person show), and an additional 21% of which have fewer than 10 employees?[1] So the majority of businesses in this country are small businesses – your businesses! Over 80% of small businesses use some kind of credit and 55% have taken out some kind of traditional loan.[2] Loans from owners and from banks are the most common sources of financing for small corporations. Unfortunately, too many small businesses rely excessively on credit cards and other forms of financing, which can actually destroy a company. You must know how to use debt financing to your benefit and be aware of the risks involved. In addition, financing providers need to have confidence that you, the small business owner, can repay the loan. This book will teach you how to instill that confidence when applying for loans and during their repayment period.

Whether your business is located in the United States or another country, one of the top five reasons for small business failure is problems with financing, which includes poor financial structure (also known as a misbalance between the owner's equity and debt money), the inability to secure financing at all, the high cost of borrowing, or even the loss of financing (when a lender or other financing provider decides to close the money tap).[3] Thus, financing is the key to every company's success. There is a tremendous amount of information on debt financing in print and on the internet. I daresay there is too much information, most of which does not focus on serving the needs of small businesses. The purpose of this book is to replace volumes of data with simple and practical recommendations and advice that will make your quest to secure a loan or financing more successful.

In this book I will guide you through the process of applying for business loans, so that you can spend more time on managing your company rather than painstakingly trying to become a loan procurement specialist. While I recommend reading the entire book, I also encourage you to skip to individual sections if you have a limited amount of time in which to find the information you need at a particular moment. Being a successful businessman or businesswoman does not mean you need to be an expert on everything. What counts is your ability to find answers now, and this book will make sure your questions are answered.

[1] US Census Bureau at www.census.gov.
[2] "Financing Pattern of Small Firms: Findings from the 1998 Survey of Small Business Finance" published by the Office of Advocacy of the U.S. Small Business Administration (SBA) in September 2003.
[3] "Reasons for Business Failure Come in Three Broad Groups" by Scott Clark; published in the Puget Sound Business Journal on July 18, 1997. "Starting a New Business: Ten Reasons New Businesses Fail" by Nic Cicutti, published on MSN Money Special.

BEFORE PREPARING A LOAN REQUEST

Chapter 1 - Simply Debt: Cons and Pros

Debt in the form of loans is something many small business owners are cautious about, even afraid of. However, I am a firm believer that debt can benefit your company and help it through various stages of its life cycle: daily operations, seasonal fluctuations, growth and expansion, acquisitions, and even start-up. In addition, debt is frequently the cheapest source of financing available to small companies. Before you even begin estimating whether your company can repay a specific loan, you should look at its risks and benefits closely. A small business owner can get carried away by looking at benefits. As a banker, I like to start with risks and move on to studying benefits only after I fully understand and become comfortable with risks. I call it "The 3-Step Risk Management Plan":

Step 1 – Understand risks and benefits
Step 2 – Determine whether benefits outweigh risks
Step 3 – Create and implement a strategy to ensure that benefits exceed risks. This Chapter will deal with Steps 1 and 2 and this book in its entirety will teach you how to implement Step 3.

Let us begin by identifying the risks of borrowing money. A conventional definition of "debt" is IOU (I Owe You) – it is an amount of money borrowed for a certain period of time with a promise to repay the principal (amount you borrow), interest, and possibly fees. I also want to define the term "equity". Equity is the money invested by a company's owner(s) or the money that was earned by a company and belongs to its owner(s). A business can be financed by either debt or equity, or most frequently by a combination of the two.

Many debt financing providers or lending institutions charge fees for approving and even for considering your loan requests. Throughout this book I will refer to individual employees of those companies interchangeably as lenders, lending officers, and loan officers. Below is a list of the key risks associated with borrowing money:

- Too much debt may render your business unable to pay principal and/or interest. This may lead to bankruptcy and the sale of your business assets.[1]
- Debt-related payments may worsen your business' situation in a bad year, as debt payments will not go away even if your company is short on cash. You may be able to renegotiate with your lender, but this is not guaranteed.
- In most cases small business loans require the personal guarantee of the owner(s). This may allow lenders to place a lien on and take possession of your personal assets.
- Lenders often ask to secure business debt with personal assets (e.g. personal residence, stocks, or bonds), if your business assets do not provide sufficient collateral. This is a step above a simple personal guarantee and gives lenders greater legal powers to go after the assets you pledge.
- If your business already has a significant amount of debt, lenders will be less and less likely to give you additional loans. In addition, a considerable amount of debt and little owner's equity will eventually lead to higher interest rates and fees.
- Lenders may impose restrictions, requiring their prior consent for some transactions, such as a change in ownership or additional financing with another lender.

Remember that debt is not a permanent source of financing and will require repayment at some point. I have seen small businesses borrow money from one lender to make payments on loans to another lender. This may postpone business failure, but will not solve the problem. Debt is good only in moderation or with some limits. An excellent example of what debt can do to your business was cited in *American City Business Journals:* "Securing business loans is like pouring water into a boat. As long as you keep it under control and pay back the debt (scooping the water back out), your business boat should be stable. However, if you obtain too much debt, you could easily debt swamp the boat and sink your business."[2]

By now you are probably asking yourself why anybody would want to take such grave risks and borrow money. Well, only a small number of businesses have enough cash provided by their owners in the form of equity investment. Remember that equity, by definition, does not require repayment, although it is certainly desired and even expected. The majority of small businesses have limited financial resources and would be out of business without loans. Here are the benefits of financing some of your assets and operations with loans.

- Lenders have no claim on your company's earnings – if your profitability goes up, you and your business keep the profits after payments of principal and interest.
- Interest is typically tax deductible, which lowers your actual cost of borrowing.
- Loan interest and related fees are typically less expensive than the cost of equity.
- When your company borrows, you continue to be its owner and are ultimately responsible for making short-term and long-term business decisions.
- Your principal and interest payments can be forecasted relatively easily. Thus your ability to make debt payments can be realistically assessed (aside from unpredictable events outside of your control, such as recession or the loss of a major customer).
- It typically takes less time to secure loans, as compared to equity financing.

All businesses require capital (cash) and cash is never ample; at least not at all times, even for very profitable companies. Debt can help small business owners to fill in the lack of capital and give you greater return on your money. I realize that many small business owners never estimate the potential return their businesses can generate when they compare different sources of financing (debt versus equity). However, this exercise does not require previous financial knowledge; it involves very basic math and it is very useful. In the table below[3] you can see the annual profit of a restaurant owner.

Take a look at the areas in bold. In Case A, the restaurant owner invested $90,000 in personal equity. In Case B, she invested $30,000.

While in Case A the "profit after tax plus the owner's salary" in dollars is greater, it is significantly less in percentage terms. Of course, more money is better and percentages may not mean much to some small business owners. However, you cannot afford to tie up an extra $60,000 that does not earn as much as it can in other business opportunities.

Year One Return	Case A	Case B
Revenue	$560,000	$560,000
Gross profit	$420,000	$420,000
Operating profit	$29,680	$29,680
Interest due	$2,166	$6,497
Principal due	$7,500	$22,500
Total annual debt payment	$9,666	$28,997
Profit after debt payment	$20,014	$683
Taxes (40%)	$8,006	$273
Profit to the owner after tax	$12,009	$410
Profit above plus salary to the owner	**$44,009**	**$32,410**
Return on profit above plus salary to the owner	**48.90%**	**108.03%**
Owner's capital (a.k.a. equity)	$90,000	$30,000
Debt (a.k.a. loans / other creditors)	$30,000	$90,000
Total business assets	$120,000	$120,000
Interest rate	8.25%	8.25%

[1] Bankruptcy law is a complicated topic, and I urge you to go through this process under the supervision of a good bankruptcy lawyer (this can be costly for a small business owner).
[2] "Debt-loan Blues" by Scott Clark; 11/19/04, American City Business Journals, Inc.
[3] This is one of many approaches to estimating profitability and return. It assumes operating profit on a cash basis and does not include depreciation/other non-cash expenses. The loan example is the term loan payable over four years. Year One does not mean the restaurant's first year in operation.

Chapter 2 – Translating Your Business Goals into Debt Financing Terms

Both small business owners and lenders often tell me that they seem to be speaking different languages and do not truly understand each other's needs. No matter how financially savvy, small business owners are close to their companies and tend to be very passionate about what they do; sometimes too passionate in the opinion of lending officers. Lenders know that passion alone does not guarantee loan repayment. In contrast, lenders are process and numbers people, even when they absolutely love their work and enjoy watching their loans make a difference to the viability of small businesses. My goal is to show you that it is not so hard to convert the business ideas closest to your heart into language lenders will understand. My strategies will not only help you reach your goals (to secure loan financing, receive better loan pricing, etc.), but they will also show you how to present your business in the best possible light.

Every lender's main goal is to extend loans to companies that can repay them. I advise my own customers to create a simple table, similar to the one presented below. On the left side you should write your company's financial and non-financial goals. Frequently such business goals will be the same as your personal goals, because many small business owners create their companies in order to achieve their aspirations and dreams. This is your time! Talk about your most important goals and capture them in up to five bullet points.

When you have completed this task, shift your attention to the right side of the table. At the top, write this sentence: "My goal is to approve loans to companies that can repay them." While you are not a lender, you will be training yourself to think like one. Here is the message lenders should hear from you: "I understand that your main responsibility is to ensure loan repayment, and here is how I am going to achieve it." Take it a step further and think of granting loans as your own small business. Keep this motto in mind when you are translating your goals into language lenders will understand. In addition, do not forget that loans are repaid from your business' cash flow. If your business idea or your company does not promise positive cash, lenders will not be excited to speak with you. In later chapters you will learn that collateral, the financial qualities of guarantors, and certain other factors may alone be sufficient to qualify for a loan. Nevertheless, start with how the accomplishment of your business and personal goals will produce positive cash flow to ensure timely loan repayment.

It is a lot easier to complete the right side of the table when you have quantitative goals such as growing your customer base to 1,000; serving at least 100 customers a day; or selling at least 100,000 books this year. However, it is not a problem if you do not have readily-available numbers – qualitative goals can be converted into numbers. Below is an example of a small real estate investment company in Silver Spring, Maryland. The owner specializes in buying and renovating rundown houses and renting them to low-income families. Rental income traditionally comes from federal government reimbursements. The owner approached a lender with a loan request to finance the acquisition of his fourth house. Here is how he translates his business goals into explanations the lender is happy to see:

Bridge Table: Translating my business goals into terms bankers can understand and appreciate

You	You as Lender: "My goal is to approve loans to companies that can repay them."
▪ Buy 4th house that will become a good source of additional cash to complement my existing real estate investments.	▪ This house will generate sufficient rent to pay for all operating expenses and bank debt with a comfortable cushion. ▪ Based on my preliminary assessments, this property will appraise at $xxx and I will meet the bank's 30% down-payment (equity investment) requirement.

▪ This real estate investment will help me become independent from my dental career and retire by the age of 50. My real estate properties can possibly offer a new, full-time career, when they produce enough excess cash to cover my family's living expenses.	▪ My dental career alone offers satisfactory cash to support my family before income from the real estate investments. I do not rely on real estate income. ▪ My present income offers excess cash flow that can be used to subsidize payments for this additional mortgage, if the house remains vacant for a period of up to 6 months.
▪ Build enough equity in investment properties that will offer cash to pay for both of my sons' college education, possibly a down payment for their own homes.	▪ If there is not enough equity in the property, I have cash savings or can offer equity in one of my existing investment properties to satisfy the bank's requirement for collateral.
▪ Rehabilitate a property that will offer a low-income family a comfortable home.	▪ The bank will receive positive publicity and credit for supporting a project that supports community investment and rehabilitation.

Here are a few guidelines on how to convert your business goals into the statements lenders want to see:

1. Establish a link between your goals, experiences, and past achievements and how these qualities will help ensure timely payments of principal and interest, comply with loan agreements, provide collateral, etc. Enhance your discussion with numbers!

2. When talking about your business, focus on your long-term horizon or at least 2 to 3 years into the future. This is necessary because lenders are not likely to want to speak with you if they sense that your business may not be around in a year or two.[1]

3. Focus on providing proof, on the basis of either historical financial results or projections, that your company can produce enough cash to make payments on the debt it already has and any additional debt you may be requesting. It is better to use historical financial results unless your company is a start-up or has recently lost money. When your request for loan financing relies on projections, make sure that you can explain your assumptions behind revenues and expenses.

I recommend making sure that your business goals can be translated into numbers – show lenders that your company will be able to repay their loans. Appendix 1 provides several examples of how small business owners and managers have translated their business and personal goals into persuasive statements. Depending on the phase of your company's development (start-up, growth, maturity, or decline), you will focus either on something you have already achieved, or are yet to achieve. The sole goal is to show lenders that you understand their needs, respect their concerns, and have what it takes to repay the loans. As you go through this book and learn more about how to secure the loans you need, you will perfect your skill of translating your goals into the statements lenders want to hear.

---

[1] Exceptions to this rule are possible when your loan request is short-term in nature and when you offer cash and other liquid collateral.

Chapter 3 – The Importance of Knowing How Much, Why, and How

The following are three examples of small business owners applying for loans, who failed to establish credibility with lenders from the very first meeting.

1. An entrepreneur with a wealth of experience in managing convenience stores approached a lender with a request to finance his own first store. This gentleman had several things lenders look for in a prospective business customer: business knowledge, a modest amount of cash available as an initial equity investment, and even a business plan indicating that all key areas were thought out in advance. A hitch arose when the lender asked this applicant how much money he wanted to borrow. The response was: "I probably need between $50,000 and $60,000. Better yet, let us make it $75,000, just in case." The lender's immediate note to himself was: "How can I trust this man's projections and ultimately his ability to repay the loan, if he does not even know how much money he needs to open his own store?" **You need to know how much you need to borrow.**

2. An owner of an existing architectural firm with about $4 million in gross revenue approached the bank with a request for a new $500,000 line of credit. Her company had an existing 3-year relationship with the bank, but had never borrowed more than $250,000. When asked to explain why she needed this amount of money, the owner confidently responded that she wanted to have some extra money to pay year-end bonuses during a traditionally slow time of the year. However, an analysis of projected financial statements that came with the loan request revealed that the company would need up to $300,000, while the loan request was for $500,000. When asked about the discrepancy, the owner was slightly surprised by the question but then explained that the remainder might be needed for unforeseen events. The lender's immediate note to himself was: "The customer is either not careful with

estimating the actual financing need or may not be telling the whole story. Do I trust the customer for whom a $200,000 difference is only a chunk of change?" **You need to know why you need to borrow.**

3. An owner of a high-end women's clothing store approached a lender with a request for a $200,000 term loan to finance the opening of her new store. She also indicated that she would be providing $50,000 in personal capital for that purpose. The lender was given a detailed 3-year budget for the new store. It seemed like a perfect addition to the three existing stores. However, the lender noticed that the explanations provided about how the $200,000 loan would be used were minimal. The expense categories, such as $50,000 for store equipment, were too broad and did not tie into the lender's familiarity with the industry. The lender also discovered that the costs of opening the last store, of similar size, just two years ago were almost half of the expected costs for the new store.

When asked about the discrepancies, the applicant responded that these were rough estimates to account for cost increases and to allow for contingencies. Moreover, the owner was requesting a loan for three years, while her own projections were showing that the company was likely to repay the loan in five. The lender's immediate note to herself was: "The customer was able to figure out the budget, but could not realistically estimate the very first cash outflow (cost of opening the store)? Not to mention a 200% increase in cost from two years ago and not knowing when her company will be able to repay the loan. Am I being given the full picture, and is the owner able to open and successfully run another store?" **You need to know how quickly your business can repay the loan and whether it can generate sufficient cash flow to repay the loan.**

I should note that these findings did not necessarily preclude these small business owners from securing the funding they sought. However, the above weaknesses certainly did not help them instill confidence in lenders that their loans will be repaid. Financial statements may indicate on paper that loans can be repaid. Nevertheless, if lenders do not believe in you, or get the impression that the numbers are not valid or that you do not know what you are doing, the opportunity to get the loan your business needs will be lost.[1]

Before you submit your loan request, you must be able to answer these four questions:

1. Why do I need the money?
2. How much money do I need?
3. How fast can I or my company repay the loan?
4. Will the company generate sufficient cash flow to repay the loan?

These four areas should be at the top of your list if you are preparing a formal request for a loan proposal, a formal business plan, a one-page summary of your company's financing needs, or even if you deliver your loan request verbally. By addressing the above issues you will achieve several goals: establish credibility in the lenders' eyes, demonstrate that you have seriously planned for this business decision, and provide documentary support of your planning efforts. Credibility is a very important part of your relationship with any lender. I am confident that my banking colleagues will agree that even when your business has the necessary cash flow and collateral, and your management team has the necessary experience to shape a successful enterprise, a lack of credibility can seriously hamper your ability to secure loans.

Banks and other financial institutions take the lending of money to small business owners seriously. Even large banks that historically overlooked this market niche have come to realize that small business loans can bring significant profits. While individual loan officers lend their companies' money, their professional reputations and jobs are on the line. Bad loans can and will get them fired. This is why lenders want to make sure that you are serious about how you will use their money. They want to make sure that you took the time to estimate your financing needs and evaluate the risks involved in supporting your company's operations with their money.

A word about projections – they do not have to include complex and extensive financial calculations. Many loan requests are pre-screened, using what is known as a back-of-the-envelope analysis (very simple financial analysis). However, all projections should be based on sound assumptions and include key elements, which are discussed later in this book.

---

[1] Remember that the inability to make your case during the very first meeting does not always mean that all hope is lost. However, focus on presenting your loan request the right way the first time. This will save you time and money in the long run.

Chapter 4 - How Much is Too Much?

How much is too much? When do loans become too much of a burden on your business and its cash flow? I am asked these questions very often by small business owners. Unless you secure your loan with cash or marketable securities, which carries the lowest risk for lenders, you need to estimate if your company can afford to pay the debt (service the debt). This includes paying interest as well as repaying the principal. Even if your loan is secured by cash collateral, why would you want to offer the cash to lenders if you are not sure that you can repay the loan and get your cash back?

So, how much debt is too much? It may be too late when you find yourself in a situation where your business is not keeping up with its agreed upon payments; when you have depleted your business cash reserves; when you have to use your personal cash to pay business debt; and when lenders call to schedule meetings to discuss their concerns about your business' financial condition. This is why I recommend creating some simple but realistic and conservative projections to estimate your company's ability to repay the loan you are about to request.

Many small business owners are not comfortable with creating their own projections or even thinking of future business finances. If this is how you feel, and you are still applying for loans, I suggest you copy the table below, enlarge it, and read it periodically for a day or two. Better yet, take a look at it together with the family members who rely on your company's income.

I dislike the financial side of business. I do not know much about it and will never become a financial guru. I resent the idea of creating even simple projections to estimate my company's ability to make loan payments.	I did not plan properly and did not estimate my business' ability to repay its loans. Now my business is on the brink of bankruptcy and lenders are going after my personal assets to get their loans repaid.

You may say that this is an extreme example. Well, bankruptcy is not so rare for small businesses. For instance, according to Dun and Bradstreet, companies with fewer than 20 employees have a 37% chance of survival in their first four years, and 10% of them will close in bankruptcy. A research paper states that 35,000 of companies closed in bankruptcy in 2003; this is equal to 6.1% of the total companies opened and 6.3% of the companies closed that year.[1] The fact is that most businesses experience cash flow problems during their lifespan, particularly younger companies. I hope that now you will not hesitate to estimate how much money your company can afford to borrow. While evaluating your company's cash flow may not be an easy task, starting and growing your business was not an easy task either, was it?

Estimate your business' possible cash flow for the next 1-2 years at the very least. It can be as easy as taking your last year's cash revenue minus cash operating expenses, if you are not expecting any growth or shrinkage. The resulting number is called operating profit and typically excludes items such as loan interest or principal payments, interest income, taxes, or any other income and expenses that do not directly relate to your business' core operations. Compare the operating profit to your expected annual debt "burden" to find out if your profits are sufficient to cover both principal and interest payments. This is a simplified way of calculating your company's cash flow. There are many approaches to analyzing your company's cash flow, but they all achieve the same purpose – allowing you to get a bird's eye view of your cash receipts minus cash expenses to help you better manage cash flow. The final goal is to estimate your company's cash available for loan repayment. We will review in greater detail how to estimate your company's cash flow for the purposes of loan repayment in Chapter 9 and 10.

There are two main approaches to estimating how much debt your business can afford to have: the Affordability and the Need Approaches (author's terms).

The Affordability Approach
Let's start with how much your company can afford to pay monthly or annually. To accomplish this goal, you will create projections and

estimate how much cash your business will have left after paying for all operating expenses. Suppose your company produces net cash from operations of $50,000, which is the money available for principal and interest payments. You plan on borrowing $200,000 over five years at 8% per year. Your annual payments will be $40,000 in principal and about $14,400 in interest for a total of $54,400. The interest payment was calculated by estimating the average outstanding principal in the middle of year multiplied by the annual interest rate. Here is the formula I used:

[principal at beginning of year − (principal payment that year / 2)] x annual interest rate

Here is how the calculations were done in this particular scenario: You know what the principal is at the beginning of the year ($200,000) and you know the amount of annual principal payment per year ($40,000). Here is how you arrive at the annual interest payment: [($200,000 − ($40,000 / 2)] x 8% = $14,400. Remember that your cash available for loan repayment is $50,000, which is less than the total payment of $54,400 due in the first year of loan repayment. Thus, your business does not appear to have enough cash even to make the first-year payment.[2] Using the same example, a term loan request for $100,000 over five years at 8% per year would have resulted in annual principal payments of $20,000 plus just over $7,000 in interest or the total of $27,000. In this case, you have a solid cushion of close to $23,000 after making loan payments, and your business should be able to afford this loan.

The Need Approach
With this method you estimate the size of the loan you need first, and then estimate your business' cash flow to figure out if your company will be able to repay it. For instance, say you would like to purchase a printing press that costs $100,000. After making inquires you find out that lenders are willing to give you a loan for up to five years at the rate of 8% and will only finance up to 70% of equipment costs, or up to $70,000. Thus, your principal payments will be $14,000, and interest payments will be just over $5,000 in the first year. Your next step is to estimate whether your company will have just over $19,000 in the first

year after the loan is approved to pay principal and interest. Remember that the loan payments should be made after all of your operating expenses have been taken care of. Otherwise, you will be dipping into the cash your company needs to survive on a day-to-day basis.

Frequently, when you seek a sizeable loan for your business and/or if your business' cash flow is tight, you will use a combination of these two approaches. They will probably look like plug-ins until you arrive at a comfortable loan amount. No matter what, keep your calculations simple. There is no need to venture into complex financial modeling. Even relatively simple estimates can provide you with an insight into how much debt is enough. Throughout this book I will continue to reiterate that your assessments must be realistic and conservative. Otherwise, you are doing a great disservice to your business, your employees, your family, and yourself. I also suggest thinking about your business' cyclicality. Cyclicality often relates to the overall economy in the country, and more importantly in the region where your company operates, as well as to your industry's condition. If you are planning to request a loan to expand your company, but it looks like the region's financial condition is starting to deteriorate and the industry already has a lot of competition, rethink your expansion plans and loan request. Of course, being an entrepreneur is all about taking risks – but ensure that the risks are calculated.

Another issue to consider is your company's seasonality. It may be dangerous to have loans that require monthly interest and even principal payments, if during certain months your company operates at a breakeven point. You should also examine your business' cash flow to look for significant fluctuations. If your company operates in an industry where returns change drastically from year to year, consider whether you have an adequate cushion to pay for your debt during the bad times. I strongly discourage the philosophy "I will deal with the problem when it comes", if there is a high probability that your company will not have the money to make loan payments and if you have no backup plan. Otherwise, you create an even bigger problem for yourself by obtaining loans. If you do decide to apply for a loan when you anticipate financial problems, determine whether you will be able to solve them and try to set aside adequate cash to help your company survive through the difficult times.

Finally, run a couple of scenarios to see what loan amount will allow you to produce the greatest return with the lowest amount of equity invested in business. Although not every small business owner estimates profits, this approach can help you ensure that you are making a financially wise financing decision. For example, suppose you are the owner of a company that manufactures and sells candles and other scented goods. You would to like to grow your business and have the option of buying new equipment. Typically, lenders will finance 70% of an equipment purchase. To grow your company's revenue by $100,000, you need to buy equipment in the amount of about $71,500 and request a loan for $50,000 (numbers are rounded). To grow your company's revenue by $200,000, you need to buy equipment in the amount of about $143,000 and request a loan for $100,000. So you can apply for a $50,000 or a $100,000 loan to increase your revenue by $100,000 or $200,000, respectively. What will your decision be? Some may say that greater revenue is better as it results in greater profits. While this is partially true, growth in revenue often needs to be supported by greater loan financing, which tends to reduce profitability. Remember that more debt means an increase in interest and principal payments.

As you can see from the table below, the smaller revenue growth in Case A offers higher dollar returns but a smaller percentage return. In addition, Case A requires less of the owner's capital and results in less outstanding debt. Case B offers lower profit but produces a higher percentage return. Furthermore, Case B calls for a larger amount of the owner's capital and greater loan financing. Of course, this is a simplified scenario, which assumes that your business' so-called profit margins hold steady and that your company's assets will grow to the extent of the new equipment purchased. Nevertheless, it is a good example of how the dollar return may be greater with less revenue growth, and that dollar and percentage return are not always correlated. You can choose to use either of these approaches. Taking the simple step of putting a few numbers together can help you avoid costly mistakes. The math that goes into these calculations is not any more sophisticated than the math you use in your daily operations.

	Most recent year	Case A	Case B
Revenue	$444,500	$544,500	$644,500
Gross profit	$266,700	$326,700	$386,700
Operating profit	**$44,450**	**$54,450**	**$64,450**
Interest due	$0	$3,713	$7,425
Principal due	$0	$10,000	$20,000
Total annual debt payment	**$0**	**$13,713**	**$27,425**
Profit after debt payment	$44,450	$40,737	$37,025
Taxes (40%)	$17,780	$16,295	$14,810
Profit to the owner after tax	$26,670	$24,443	$22,215
Profit above plus salary to the owner[3]	$86,670	$84,443	$82,215
Owner's return of capital invested	**69.24%**	**96.44%**	**125.12%**
Owner's capital (a.k.a. equity)	$60,008	$81,436	$102,865
Debt (a.k.a. loans)	$162,243	$212,243	$262,243
Total business assets	$222,250	$293,679	$365,107
Interest rate		8.00%	8.00%
New loan		**$50,000**	**$100,000**

[1] "Small Business: Causes of Bankruptcy", fall 2004, Don B. Bradley and Chris Cowdery of University of Central Arkansas.

[2] Of course, this is a simplified but reasonable and reliable approach. This is what finance professionals call the back-of-the-envelope approach, which tells you whether your business is likely to default on the loan.

[3] Salary to the owner was assumed to be $60,000 in the most recent year and in Cases A and B.

CHAPTER 5 - DO YOU NEED A LOAN PROPOSAL?

Before answering this question, let's look at one of several possible definitions of a "Request for Loan Proposal" or RLP. The term stems from the Request for Proposal or RFP, which is nothing more than a request for a bid or a quote from a person or a business entity. In the case of a request for loan proposal, you are asking a lender or several lenders to consider your request for a loan and give you their best loan proposals. There are many shapes an RLP can take. It may range from a simple one-page summary of your basic loan needs to a several-page document that also includes information about you and your business, analyzes your company's financial statements, and contains other information that can help you secure the requested loan with the best possible interest rates and terms. The more thorough your request is, the greater your chances are for a favorable decision.

Do you need a formal RLP? The answer is yes and no. It all depends on how established and financially strong your business is. If your company has strong cash flow that can support payments for the requested and existing loans, banks and other financial institutions will be going after your business, trying to steal your loan relationships from each other. I have personally participated in the approval of loans where a verbal request and two to three years of historical financial statements were sufficient to approve even seven-figure loans. Unfortunately, small businesses are rarely flush with cash. Usually the opposite is the case – cash flow is frequently tight and loans are a vital source of financing operations. Therefore, an RLP may be the key element that allows you to secure loan approval.

I often compare RLP with business plans. Some businesses do not have and do not need formal business plans, while others will greatly benefit from them. The businesses that can benefit from a business plan are start-ups, financially-weak companies, or companies with limited chances of securing loan or equity financing. There are, however, examples of many successful enterprises for which business plans were not prepared[1], even when they were looking for financing. A business plan is a mere reflection of the efforts you, the business owner, put into the planning of your business, and it is your opportunity to demonstrate that you are prepared to anticipate and address potential problems.[2]

Where the RLP differs from the business plan is in its particular focus on your company's financing needs, your business' financial qualities, the qualities of your management team, an assessment of your company's risks and how you, the business owner, are qualified and plan on mitigating those risks. The RLP is nearly a very concise version of the business plan. It articulates your loan needs and expected repayment plan, discusses your business' challenges and opportunities, and demonstrates how you are prepared to ensure successful repayment of the loan. Many business plans fail to address a business' financial strengths and weaknesses and, as a result, fail to help business owners obtain the financing they seek. The RLP is designed to focus on describing your business' financial performance. However, a financial analysis of small businesses can and should be quite simple. This task can be tackled by small business owners who have only minimal familiarity with financial concepts. The RLP strategies described in this book have only one goal – to help you define your financing needs and persuade lenders that you can repay the borrowed money.

Prior to discussing the direct benefits of creating a Request for Loan Proposal, I would like to share with you some of the drawbacks. One of the key drawbacks is that an unskillfully prepared request for a loan proposal can lead potential lenders to believe that you and your business do not deserve the loans. If your RLP is not focused, lenders may conclude that you will not be able to focus on managing your business or repay the loans. Some of the other potential PLR weaknesses are:
- Focus on issues that have nothing to do with the loan request
- A lack of information about your specific financing needs (request without a request)
- A lack of an assessment of your company's financial condition
- Analysis or projections that are too optimistic
- A lack of proof that your company can cover the expected debt payments

- A lack of basic background information about you and your business

The benefit of the RLP is that it presents your request in a way that will help lenders make loan decisions quickly and efficiently. Its purpose is to gather and organize the information lenders will need in making loan decisions and exclude everything that will hurt your chances of receiving loans. A good RLP will show that you understand the financial condition of your business and its cash flow. Furthermore, it will show how the loan you are requesting will affect your company's finances. You can and should discuss some key risks and weaknesses involved in running your company and how you are prepared to mitigate them. This will give your lenders a sense of assurance in granting you the funds you are requesting. Last but not least, a well-prepared RLP may show you that requesting a specific loan may not be in the best interest of your business. After all, debt financing and, therefore, debt payments in excess of a certain amount is not for every business. The following sections aim to teach you how to prepare a powerful and effective Request for Loan Proposal that will focus on your company's financial characteristics and financing needs.

---

[1] "Does Business Plan Matter" article by Mary Baechler, Inc magazine, February 1996.
[2] "The Fine Art of Writing a Business Plan" Inc magazine, December 1999.

Chapter 6 – A Quick Overview of Financial Concepts That are Useful in Applying for Loans

The three main financial statements are: 1) income statement; 2) statement of cash flow; and 3) balance sheet. You will use them to capture your company's financial performance, and lenders use them to determine whether a loan request should be granted. These financial statements may vary in presentation from company to company and from industry to industry. However, each has the same purpose. If you feel that you have a good understanding of financial statements and banking terminology, you may skip the next two chapters.

Income Statement

An income statement, also known as a profit and loss statement or P&L statement, is a report that shows the income (sales or revenue) and expenses your business is generating. Its purpose is to show the profit or loss your business produced within a particular period of time. An income statement can cover a year, a month, a week, or even a day. The profits or losses of a business are often referred to as its bottom line. It is not only important to track and manage your profitability in each period, but it is also crucial to analyze your company's profitability trends over two or more equal periods of time. This is what lenders do when they consider your loan requests. A very basic, summary income statement is presented below. It follows a simple formula: income minus expenses equals net profit.

Income (revenue, sales)	$100,000
- Expenses	-$80,000
Net profit (net income)	**$20,000**

A more detailed version of the income statement is presented in Appendix 2. An income statement shows lenders the company's revenue trends and which products and services generate revenue. It details your business expenses, which can consist of "costs of goods sold" (expenses that can be directly related to certain sales) and operating expenses (expenses such as rent, office supplies, and administrative help, that cannot be directly traced to sold products or services). Income statement items then flow into the statement of cash flow.

Statement of Cash Flow

A statement of cash flow is the most important financial statement for lenders. Lenders traditionally begin calculating your cash flow by analyzing the income statement, because the income statement provides the foundation for the statement of cash flow. However, it is the statement of cash flow that tells lenders whether your company is likely to be able to repay loans. This statement shows all of your company's cash inflows (receipts of cash) and cash outflows (payments of cash). Below is a simplified example of a cash flow statement.

Total cash receipts	$90,000
- Total cash disbursements	-$84,000
Net cash flow	**$6,000**

Appendix 3 offers a glance at a more detailed version of the cash flow statement. The statement is derived from your income statement and balance sheet. Frequently, your accountant will prepare the cash flow statement as part of your financial statement preparation.

Balance Sheet

A balance sheet summarizes all physical and non-physical resources (assets) your company possesses. Your business assets are acquired or financed by liabilities or equity. Debt can be owed to lenders, suppliers, and even employees. Equity typically finances some of the business assets that are not financed by debt. A simple balance sheet is presented below. A balance sheet consists of two sides: the assets of your company on one side and the liabilities (debt and other money owed) and equity on the other side. The two sides must always be equal (assets equal liabilities plus equity). Your business assets can only be financed by liabilities and equity.[1]

Assets		Liabilities	
Cash	$10,000	Loan payable	$20,000
Accounts receivable	$30,000	Accounts payable	$30,000
Fixed assets (building, equipment, etc.)	$25,000	Owners' equity	$15,000
Total assets	$65,000	Total liabilities and equity	$65,000

The relationship between the above three statements is presented below. Data taken from your company's income statement and balance sheet flows into the cash flow statement and connects back to the balance sheet and the income statement. While many people find accounting tedious, it makes sense and is highly logical. **Everything starts with your cash balance** on hand in the beginning of the year. After you compile your company's income statement to reflect what happened during the year and show how your assets changed during the same period, all cash inflows and outflow **will reconcile to your cash balance at the end of the year**. The picture below presents the full circle that describes financial events in your company.

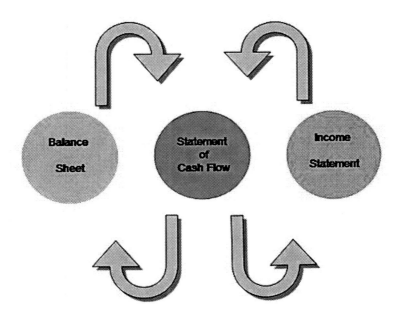

The lender may ask whether your company's financial statements are cash or accrual basis. To prepare you for this possibility, the following are explanations of these terms.

Accrual versus cash basis income statements

This concept refers to how revenues and expenses are recognized and recorded in income statements. Cash basis is prevalent among small businesses and the majority of banks are comfortable with accepting such reports. In cash income statements, you record revenue or sales when you receive payments. For example, you sell electronic equipment, but your commercial customers have an option to pay within 30 days after the delivery is made. Thus, in a cash basis statement you will not add the amount of sale to your total sales earned until the cash is collected. The same applies to expenses. Until your expenses are actually paid, you do not record them.

Unlike cash statements, accrual principal requires you to recognize your business' revenue when it is earned, not when cash is received. Suppose you sell subscriptions to an industry publication. You sell annual subscriptions for one year and receive payments for the entire year immediately. However, the accrual principle dictates that you earn your money on a pro-rata basis month by month. You recognize 1/12th of the annual revenue only as each month of the year passes. Expenses are not recorded when cash is actually paid but are recognized in relation to earned revenue. Suppose you buy and pay for raw materials twice every year. However, you use raw materials every day to manufacture goods, not just twice a year. Thus, you recognize a portion of those expenses on an ongoing basis, tying them to sales of goods.

The purpose of accrued financial statements is "to report in any given period revenue earned during the period and to report expenses that are matched against that revenue."[2] Bankers prefer accrued financial statements because they avoid drastic fluctuations in profits from year to year. For instance, you may receive much more cash than you spend in one year and spend much more than you receive in another. The accrual income statements smooth things out and avoid significant fluctuations in profits from year to year. They help lenders compare your revenue as it is earned with only those expenses that are related to the earned revenue.

---

[1] There are financing products that have features of both debt and equity, but I have almost never seen them used by small businesses.

[2] *The McGraw-Hill 36-Hour Accounting Course* by Robert Dixon and Harold Arnett, 3rd edition, 1993.

Chapter 7 – Lending Terminology and Concepts for Small Business Owners

Type of financing versus the financing institution
The number of small business loan or credit products can be overwhelming. This is because lenders often use different names for their products and services as a way to distinguish their companies' products and services from the competition. To quickly understand what is offered, first ask yourself what kind of loan product it is (see below). Is it a loan product that requires repayment? Occasionally equity financing providers can make their products look like loans, but in reality it is plain equity financing that is given in exchange for ownership in your company. Second, find out if the lender is a bank, a credit card company, a financial services company, or something else. Confusion will be eliminated: you know what product you are looking at and know the type of company that offers it. See Chapter 27 for more details.

Short-term versus long-term loan products
Short-term generally means loans that are due and/or expire within one year. Long-term loans have a term of over one year. Short-term loan products traditionally include time notes, lines of credit, and one-year term loans. Long-term loans include multi-year term loans and lines of credit, mortgages, and multi-year leases.

Loan Products

While it may seem that there are dozens of loan products offered to small business owners, those products are typically variations of a few common loan types. The most common types of loans are lines of credit, time notes, letters of credit, term loans, mortgage loans, and leases. They are discussed below.

Line of credit – Lines of credit are usually granted for a period of up to one year, although some lenders may offer lines of credit for up to three, and even five, years. These loans act just like credit cards: the more you borrow, the less you have available to borrow; when you reduce your loan balance, your amount available to borrow increases. They are commonly known as revolving lines of credit – they revolve up and down depending on your borrowing pattern. Typically, they are used to fund short-term cash flow needs, including the financing of inventory purchases and providing cash before accounts receivable are collected. You are usually charged monthly interest payments, and no principal repayments are required until the loan expires. The presumption is that you will repay your line of credit prior to its expiration.

Lines of credit may also require repayment of the line balance to $0 for a period of 30 days each year. Problems arise when small business owners cover business losses by borrowing on a line of credit instead of putting in more equity and repaying the principal on the line of credit. Lines of credit can have a demand feature and are known as demand lines of credit. Demand lines of credit do not usually have expiration dates, but the lender can demand that you repay the loan balance at any time at his or her discretion.

Time note – Time notes are non-revolving loans that mature in less than twelve months. Principal repayment is not due until the loan matures, when the loan is due in full. In the meantime, you will only pay monthly interest. Time notes are usually used for large, one-time expenses such as year-end bonuses to your employees or the acquisition of a sizeable lot of inventory offered by a supplier going out of business. While the bank may allow you to roll over one time note into another (the equivalent of refinancing), you ought to make sure that your business can generate enough cash internally to repay this loan when it is due. Otherwise, use another loan product when there is a high probability that you will not have sufficient funds to repay the time note at maturity. A variation of a time note is a discount note. The interest is charged up front, reducing the amount of proceeds you receive. As interest is charged in the beginning, it benefits the bank and your actual or effective interest rate happens to be a bit higher than the one stated in the loan agreement. However, for small business loans this difference is usually not significant.

Letter of credit – The most common loans are standby letters of credit and documentary or trade letters of credit. This product is designed to guarantee payment to your landlord, supplier, and other creditors, if your business cannot make a payment. The financial institution that issues a letter of credit on your behalf is substituting your promise to pay with its own promise to pay. This provides necessary assurance to creditors. The lending institution that gives you a letter of credit will go after your company to collect the money. There are differences in standby and documentary letters of credit: standby letters of credit are not designed to be used for payment and are therefore called standby. They are a just-in-case proof that there is money your creditor can tap into. Documentary letters of credit are designed to be used for payment, often to overseas creditors. Those creditors might not have confidence that your check will be good, and instead they ask for a documentary letter of credit from a bank or financial institution with a high credit rating. Letters of credit typically have annual fees associated with them (1-2% of the total). Normally, you will either secure your lender's letter of credit by cash or have it issued against your line of credit, in which case a line of credit has to be approved first.

Term loan – While term loans can be granted for one year, they are usually given for up to five or even seven years. These loans are non-revolving and you will be required to pay both principal and interest. As you repay this loan, you cannot borrow more like you can with a line of credit. The typical purposes of the term loan are to buy equipment, finance a partner buy-out, pay for a building or leasehold improvements, and other needs that require a large, one-time payment that can be repaid within five to seven years. Note that some lenders offer loans that combine features of the line of credit and the term loan, and they will explain how those types of loans work.

Mortgage loan – Similar to residential mortgages, business or commercial mortgages are granted to businesses to buy real estate properties. These properties can be fully or partially occupied by your company (owner-occupied) or can be used for investment properties (non-owner-occupied). Commercial mortgage loans can usually be granted for up to ten years with amortization for up to twenty-five years (see term versus amortization explanation in this chapter). You typically pay monthly principal and interest.

Lease – A form of financing for various types of equipment, leases are commonly divided into finance, or capital leases and true, or operating leases. Finance leases are similar to term loans used for equipment purchases. By choosing a finance lease you take possession of equipment at the end of the loan term. Usually only the interest portion of your payments are tax deductible. Operating leases typically allow you to apply the entire lease payments to reduce your income and therefore taxes. However, you have no ownership claim at the end of the lease term. Lease financing can have various tax consequences for businesses, and you should consider contacting a tax adviser to determine which lease type will have a greater benefit for your company. Not every lender offers lease financing. This is a market niche for a handful of large banks and specialized finance companies.

Useful Terminology

Borrower
A borrower is a person or a legal entity that borrows or receives a loan from a lender, which can be an institution or an individual.

Guarantor
A guarantor is a person or a legal entity that promises to repay the entire loan, or a portion of it, should the borrower default on payments. The guarantor cannot also be a borrower for the same loan. The concept of the guarantor is similar to co-signing for a loan. The guarantee can be limited to a certain dollar amount, or unlimited. In the same context, a recourse loan means that the lender can go after the guarantor's other assets if the loan is not paid. In the non-recourse loan, there are no guarantors and therefore the lender has no recourse.

Financing business needs with appropriate loan products
A financially prudent small business owner should strive to finance short-term cash needs with short-term loans, and long-term needs with

long-term loans. For instance, the financing of inventory purchases, accounts receivable, and other daily operations should be done with short-term loans such as lines of credit. Business acquisitions, purchases of equipment or buildings, and renovations should be financed with term loans and mortgages. This is called the matching principal. The core of this approach is that the loan term should not be longer than the useful or economic life of an asset. For example, inventory purchases should not be financed with a three-year term loan as inventory will likely be sold in less than a year (sometimes in days or weeks) but the loan will not be fully repaid. Another example is financing the acquisition of a building with a short-term loan. Would you want to finance the building purchase with a one-year line of credit, just to go through the trouble of refinancing in the following year and the year after?

Term vs. amortization

The term of the loan means the period of time within which your loan is due in full, unless of course you repay the loan prior to its maturity. Amortization is related to how your monthly principal payments are calculated. For example, a mortgage loan may have a term of five years but amortize over twenty years. Longer amortization means that you can spread your principal repayment over a longer period of time, making your monthly payments lower. However, a five-year term means that the loan will mature in five year with a significant principal balance yet to be paid. Often, the same lender will then review your company's performance and renew or refinance your loan for another five years, keeping your monthly payments at about the same level as they were. Why would lenders want to complicate their lives and require the mortgage term to be less than amortization? To protect themselves. If in five years the lender notices that your company's financial performance has deteriorated, the lender has the option of refusing to refinance the mortgage. You will then be forced to look for another lender because the loan will be due in full.

Straight-line versus mortgage-style amortization

This concept is applicable to term loans and mortgages where principals and interest payments are involved. Straight line means you pay equal principal payments plus interest on the outstanding loan balance. For instance, a $20,000 term loan for five years with equal monthly principal payments will call for $333.33 in monthly principal. The interest will vary based on the loan balance. Interest is typically calculated on the outstanding loan balance and is higher in the beginning. Thus, your total monthly payments will vary and are more difficult to predict. Straight-line amortization is synonymous with equal monthly principal payments. Please note that some lenders may offer quarterly and annual payment options, but monthly payments are the most common.

Mortgage-style amortization aims to offer equal total monthly payments that include pre-calculated principal *and* interest. A portion of your payment will go toward principal and the rest toward interest. The proportional relationship between principal and interest will change throughout the life of your loan (with significantly more interest in the beginning, more principal at the end). Nevertheless, the total monthly payments will always stay the same and are easier to predict. Mortgage-style amortization is synonymous with equal monthly payments.

Collateral
Collateral means assets lenders will go after if you default on repayment, in an attempt to recover the amount you borrowed. Collateral may include "real", or tangible, and intangible assets. In the event that you default on your loans, lenders will be able to take possession of those assets and sell them to repay the loans. Lenders frequently take a lien on all business assets of your company, which include accounts receivable, inventory, equipment, furniture and fixtures, and other assets. However, at times lenders will agree to take a lien on a specific, single asset such as a particular piece of equipment or a real estate property, without taking a lien on all business assets.

Eligible versus ineligible collateral
The only way to find out what collateral you can borrow against is by asking your prospective lender. For instance, lenders lend against accounts receivable that have been outstanding for less than 90 days. In addition, when your inventory is highly salable, advance rates are likely to be higher. For instance, you are not likely to get loans using

fresh produce as collateral, but should be able to borrow against an inventory of salable books. You will have to work with your lender to secure the desired advance rates.

Advance rate

Advance rates are used by lenders to allow businesses to borrow on a line of credit using accounts receivable, inventory, real estate, and some other assets as collateral. In addition, you are likely to hear this term when financing the purchase of equipment with a term loan. The assets are used as collateral and create availability to borrow. Advance rates do vary from lender to lender; however, general industry practices advise lenders to lend up to 80% of the value of some accounts receivable, up to 50% of certain inventory, up to 80% of the value of some equipment, and up to 80% of certain appraised value of real estate.

Covenants

Covenants are financial or non-financial conditions that have to be met during the term of your loan. They are measurable and will be tested at certain intervals. Examples of covenants include certain minimum EBITDA (earnings before interest, tax, depreciation, and amortization) that need to be met either annually or quarterly. Another example is maintaining a certain amount in equity or net worth in the company during each period or at all times. Non-financial covenants may include the submission of monthly accounts receivable aging reports or quarterly business financial statements. Before you agree to any covenants, you should assess whether your company is able to meet them.

Financial reporting requirements

Financial reporting refers to a list of financial statements that you will be required to provide on a regular basis. For example, you may be required to provide business tax returns, accountant-prepared financial statements (compiled, reviewed, or audited), personal financial statements, and personal tax returns. Reviewed and audited financial statements may be quite costly to prepare. In addition, when consenting to providing a financial statement you have to make sure that you can do it in a timely manner.

Underwriting
Underwriting is the process of considering your loan request, making a decision, and booking your loan, if it is approved.

Scored underwriting
The style of underwriting used in the approval of small business loans. Lenders utilize proprietary statistical software programs that require certain data about your business. This may include the number of years your company has been in business, its liquidity[1], its leverage[2], and other information. Your company will then be assigned a score, which is derived by comparing the information about it to the pool of information taken from other businesses. That score helps determine whether the loan will be given to your business. This approach is used in analyzing loan requests up to $250,000 in some larger financial institutions. Smaller banks are less likely to use a scoring method.

Loan-to-value (LTV)
This concept typically applies to mortgage loans. Loan-to-value or LTV is calculated by the following formula: mortgage loan divided by the property's appraised value. Lenders will often lend up to 70%-80% of LTV.

Appraisal (real estate, equipment, inventory, other)
The appraisal is a process that assigns value to a particular asset so it can be used as collateral. Lenders usually do not require appraisals and use values reported in your companies' financial statements. However, when lenders need additional assurance that collateral has certain value, they may require an appraisal. Borrowers commonly pay for the cost of appraisals.

Field examination
A field exam is an audit of your internal bookkeeping, procedures, and specific collateral. Exams are commonly required by lenders for larger loans, as those exams tend to be costly. The costs are covered by borrowers. Lenders usually require field exams for asset-based loans.

Term sheet vs. commitment letter

A term sheet is an outline of key conditions on which a lender is likely to lend you money. A term sheet is not a guarantee or a promise to lend. It is used to initiate discussion and negotiate the terms of a loan. A commitment letter is a commitment to lend based on outlined conditions. To confirm your willingness to accept the lender's conditions and move toward the loan closing, you have to sign this document by a specified date. Some banks may use the two documents interchangeably; please read both documents thoroughly to make sure that you understand the conditions and responsibilities they impose.

Fixed versus floating rates

Lenders offer either floating or fixed rates. Floating rates benefit lenders when the interest rates are expected to increase. Your interest rate can be tied to the prime rate (often the *Wall Street Journal* prime rate), Federal Home Loan rates, U.S. government treasury bonds, and LIBOR rates (London Interbank Offered Rate). All you need to know is that the rates can fluctuate over time and your interest expense will vary based on the loan amount outstanding and the interest rate in effect. Fixed rates do not change. They are particularly useful when you expect interest rates to go up and when your loan term is very long (as for mortgage loans). With fixed interest rates you will not, however, be able to enjoy lower pricing that will be available, if interest rates decline. Your rate is fixed, unless you refinance your loan or negotiate a rate change with your lender.

---

[1] Liquidity is typically measured by current or quick ratios and the amount of net working capital.

[2] Leverage is typically measured by "total liabilities / net worth" or "total liabilities / tangible net worth" and by the dollar amount of tangible net worth.

PREPARING A LOAN REQUEST
(CASH FLOW FACTORS)

CHAPTER 8 - ANALYZING YOUR HISTORICAL FINANCIAL PERFORMANCE AND STAYING ONE STEP AHEAD OF LENDERS

To manage a financially successful small business you should have a good knowledge of your company cash flow at any point of time. This is what lenders are looking for. To be frank, I have seen a number of small business loans extended to businesses whose owners did not demonstrate sound financial knowledge. However, many of those companies were established operations and showed a track-record of sufficient cash flow to repay the loans. Their historical cash flow showed a sufficient cushion to cover debt payments in the event of a downturn and declining profits. In addition, there was often a person other than the owner who was in charge of the company's financial affairs. Problems in dealing with lenders begin when a business' cash flow does not allow any margin for error and the company cannot afford to have a bad year financially.

I recall a customer of my bank, a company that designed exhibits for various New England expos. The company was owned by one individual, who employed two full-time and three part-time employees. The bank was lending money to the company for short periods of time to help finance work prior to the beginning of those expos. Loans were repaid after each job was completed. Some of the loans were occasionally "rolled" into new loans and the company's overall debt grew from $30,000 to over $300,000 in about seven years. However, the owner was always able to pay interest and justify to the bank that he would be able to repay the principal. Profits were modest, but the principal was able to draw $50,000 to $60,000 in total compensation each year.

Unfortunately, after a series of incorrectly priced projects and resulting cost overruns, eventually the owner was unable to pay even the interest. The end of this story was not happy. The business owner had to sell his house to repay the bank's debt and, after many years of being his own boss, he was forced to apply for a job himself. This fiasco could have easily been avoided if the owner had looked at his company's financial statements in the way I have outlined. He would have realized that his company had taken on too much debt and any unexpected drop in profit might result in failure to make loan payments.

Why do you need to analyze your company's historic financial performance and cash flow? The answer is quite simple – this is something lenders will do. There is no better way to prepare for their questions and anticipate some of their actions than by doing the same analysis, which is often very simple. Before lenders give you money, they want to know that you know where your business stands financially. Your goal is also to demonstrate that you have good book-keeping and record-keeping practices. Going through the exercise of reviewing your financial statements prior to applying for a loan is bound to earn lenders' praise. This is particularly important as lenders often review more than one loan request per day and you are sure to stand out if you do your homework before applying. Be prepared to provide two to three years of financial statements, if your company has been in business that long, and comment on the trends. In addition, focus on addressing negative changes in those trends, as most lenders will focus more on negatives than on positives.

An example: a prospective customer is requesting a $260,000 loan to purchase a liquor license and finance renovations to move her existing restaurant to a new location. The existing restaurant has been in business for about seven years – so the bank requested the three most recent tax returns. As an analyst, the first thing I did was to summarize the information in those returns by entering the restaurant's historical financial data into summary tables, which lenders call "spreads". See Appendix 4 for details. (Notice that next to the amount columns the software conveniently included percentages because changes in dollar amounts do not always give the complete picture.)

What lenders are likely to see in the income statement

In the income statement, lenders focus on analyzing operating profitability. The restaurant's operating profit declined significantly in 2001 and a bit more in 2002. By looking at the top of the income statement, I noticed that revenue declined substantially in 2001, although it recovered slightly in the most recent year. Expect questions on revenue declines, on what you have done to improve the situation, and on what you are doing to make sure that improvement continues. Also notice a percentage change in gross profits. It actually improved over three years, which means that something happened to decrease the costs of food, alcohol, and direct labor. Operating expenses showed that employee salaries and benefits continued to grow despite lower sales, which certainly warrants a question about why the owner did not reduce staffing levels in response to lower sales.

Some discussion is typically devoted to the owners' distributions (withdrawals of cash). Many small business owners report business profit (or loss) on their personal tax returns and have to pay taxes based on their personal tax bracket. As a result, they have to withdraw or distribute some percentage of business net income to cover those taxes. Furthermore, in some instances less financially savvy owners take out all the earnings, which is the cash necessary for the daily operations of their businesses. They view salaries and distributions as compensation they are entitled to. In this particular case, the owner has been withdrawing as much as, or even more than the net income earned during the year. As some of you may know, net income reported in the income statement does not always equal cash earned by your company. However, to simplify our discussion, I am assuming that the difference is not material.

Withdrawing all the profits from the company is not generally considered to be a good practice, although lenders see it happen all the time. Remember one thing: if you withdraw all of the earnings out of your business each year, lenders may want to analyze your personal cash flow and liquid assets to ensure that you do not spend all that money. If you withdraw most of the earnings from your business on a regular basis, but your personal assets (e.g. investment and deposit accounts, real estate) do not increase at a similar rate, lenders will want to know what happens to all that cash. What lenders are looking for is in a sense an implied assurance that you can put some of that cash back into the company or reduce your future earnings distributions to make debt payments.

This was a brief overview of some of the most common things lenders are likely to focus on when considering a loan application. Some lending officers may even analyze all the items on the income statement line by line, but they typically do not have the luxury of time to discuss them all with you. Thus, focus on reviewing your operating profits, trends in general accounts such as revenues, gross and operating profits, owners' distributions, and trends in percentages terms. In addition, be prepared to explain deteriorations, declining trends, and any sizeable fluctuations.

What lenders are likely to see in the balance sheet

Balance sheet analysis can be somewhat tricky, as balance sheets can vary significantly from one small business to another; in my experience balance sheets may vary even more significantly than income statements. I recommend focusing on liquid assets and owners' equity or net worth.

The most liquid assets are your cash and marketable securities (e.g. stocks or bonds). Less liquid are accounts receivable and inventory. Liquidity is often measured by comparing the sum of your company's cash, marketable securities, inventory, and accounts receivable to the sum of principal payments and loans due within one year, accounts payable, and accruals. In Appendix 4, there is an example of the same restaurant whose cash has been dwindling over a three-year period. You may realize that it was due to declining profits, the owner taking distributions in excess of earnings, the continuing need to make debt payments, and voluntary reductions in bank notes payable. Voluntary reduction in the line of credit balance is a good thing in the long term. However, the company is approaching the point where its cash cushion will disappear, leaving it without the funds to cover unexpected emergencies.

The owners' equity in the business is another area of focus. As you will notice, in the example shown the restaurant's net worth has remained stable over the last three years. Lenders try to calculate your business' true net worth or equity. They call it tangible net worth. This is achieved by subtracting so-called intangible assets (e.g. goodwill) from the business' net worth. Intangible assets are essentially an accounting entry – assets that have value only in your company's financial statements. Unlike inventory, equipment, and even accounts receivable, intangible assets are likely to offer no value to lenders. See Chapter 12 for more information on intangible assets. When you subtract the intangible assets listed on the balance sheet of the restaurant from its total equity, you will be left with very little, even negative, equity. This is what lenders call tangible net worth. Some of the ways of mitigating lack of equity in the business are by offering additional collateral (only if you are asked) or by offering your personal guarantee, if you have sizeable personal investments. In this particular case the owner could not offer either. As a result, the lender approved the loan after obtaining a guarantee from the SBA (Small Business Administration).

Of course, financial or credit analysis of your company's operations can be more complex, but you will be far ahead of other small business owners if you begin focusing on and addressing at least some of the issues discussed here. In addition, you will have more credibility in your conversations with lenders even in situations where your company's financial performance is sub-par. Be realistic when looking at your company's financial strengths and weaknesses. Remember, if you appear to be out of touch with reality you cannot make a persuasive case to a lender.

CHAPTER 9 - EVALUATING YOUR CASH FLOW BASED ON HISTORICAL VERSUS PROJECTED FINANCIAL STATEMENTS

There is limited statistical data available to show how many loans are approved based on historical financial statements versus projections or expected future performance. However, based on my experience in lending to small businesses, the overwhelming majority of loans are approved based on historical financial statements. In many cases owners provide projections in addition to historical financial statements, but historical financial reports are the true basis for loan decisions. Does this mean that lenders do not lend based on projections? Yes, they do, but in such instances they look much more closely at the personal assets of the principals and most of the time require their personal guarantees. Moreover, with only projections to back up your loan request, you should be sure that your management and trade experience in the field are sufficient to assure lenders that you are a suitable risk.

Why would lenders want to lend based on past financial results that may not be repeated in the future? The answer is simple – if you have already established a track record, it is easier to see that you can run a successful company. This approach has proven to be effective, although not error-proof, and lenders are not likely to change the way they do business anytime soon.

When lenders assess your company's ability to repay loans, they create a document called the statement of business cash flow. Note that this statement is probably different from the cash flow statement prepared by your accountant. Here I offer an approach widely used by bankers. Remember that the goal is to estimate whether your company can repay loans. This method allows you to evaluate your business cash flow in a way that is similar to your prospective lending officers' method. In Appendix 5 I show you step by step how to analyze your business' ability to repay existing and future loan obligations. To fill in the data, you will need to have your business' income statement and balance sheet. Although this process may appear intimidating, it is very simple and mechanical. If you are not comfortable making the calculations, your accountant or another person with a financial background should be able to help you with these calculations.

A lender's goal is to reasonably and conservatively calculate your company's operating cash flow, which accounts for daily operations (revenue minus operating expenses), non-cash expenses such as depreciations expense, owners' distributions, taxes, investments in so-called fixed assets (e.g. equipment, building), and loans or equity investments used to finance those fixed assets. The net figure is then compared to your company's historical scheduled debt payment. Lenders will use the most recent year's operating cash flow as a watermark for estimating whether your business can make future expected debt payments.

The example shown in Appendix 5 is a wholesaler of fresh fruit and vegetables. As you can see, operating profits have historically been slim, while investments in fixed assets (mostly the purchase of and major updates to equipment) have been quite significant. Once depreciation expense or a non-cash item is added back, lenders begin to get a better idea of a company's cash flow. Notice that no loans were used to purchase fixed assets, which means that the company was strong enough financially to finance its assets internally. Unfortunately, the company's operating cash flow in the last two years was negative, even before making small interest payments on a line of credit. The owner was in the habit of paying himself a rather high salary, substantially more than his family needed, while minimizing his company's operating profits. Note that the salary information was obtained from the income statement and is included in the operating profit number.

The owner approached a bank with a loan request to help finance the sale of the company to his nephew, who had already been involved in the business for many years. The key reason why the bank was able to approve the loan request was because the existing owner was clearly able to demonstrate that his salary could be reduced by at least $150,000 without affecting his lifestyle. In addition, the nephew's experience running the company and his willingness to limit his salary were contributing factors. Without these mitigating factors, I doubt the bank would have been interested in extending the loan. This is why I recommend analyzing your company's historical cash flow and planning for it to be the basis of your loan request.

Does this mean that if you have a start-up company without historical financial statements or a company with weak financial results in the last year or two that you will not be able to secure the loan financing you need? Not necessarily, particularly if you do your homework. First and foremost, your projections have to be realistic and conservative. Time after time I see small business owners who paint a rosy picture, which lenders are trained to be skeptical about. If your projections are too optimistic, lenders will reduce your projected figures. Moreover, you will lose credibility. Thus, projections should be based on realistic assumptions. These assumptions should be explained and justified. Do not forget about putting your efforts into meeting those projections. A customer of mine, a $5 million general contractor in Massachusetts, prepared projections for several years and fell behind the estimates each time. He continued to take out loans, while there were clear signals that his expected profits were too optimistic. Needless to say, after a few losses, the bank chose to let this customer go. The conclusion is simple – be realistic.

Lenders frequently compare your company to others in the same industry. Make sure that your income statement and balance sheet[1] (if you decide to prepare one) are comparable to those of the competition. This is particularly crucial for small business owners who rely on projections in applying for loans. If they vary significantly, particularly in a negative way, a lender may ask you to explain the differences. After all, the dynamics of operating in the same industry lead to similarities in financial statements. Lenders often utilize the industry financial statements compiled in the Risk Management Association's Annual Statement Studies. Banks from all around the United States submit financial data from their borrowers (without disclosing their customers' identities), and the RMA puts them together to help lenders make prudent loan decisions. While not every industry is covered in that publication, you may want to compare your data and ratios with those provided by RMA.[2] This will allow you to identify differences and anticipate lenders' questions.

---

[1] Note that for start-up loans, lenders frequently require a so-called opening or beginning balance sheet. If your company has been in business for several years, in some cases lenders would want to see income statement projections or cash budget projections, not a balance sheet, which simply means less work for you.

[2] If you already have a business relationship with a bank or a financial institution, ask your account officer whether he or she has a copy of the RMA Annual Statement Studies. All you need is a copy of the page for your industry.

CHAPTER 10 – DETERMINING YOUR FINANCING NEEDS: HOW MUCH YOU NEED VERSUS HOW MUCH YOU CAN AFFORD

As I mentioned in Chapter 4, you can either determine how much you need (the Need Approach) or how much you can afford (the Affordability Approach) to estimate your chances of being granted a loan. When you do not assess your business' ability to repay the debt, you take a significant risk of obtaining a loan you may not be able to repay. The calculations are rather simple and do not require an exorbitant amount of time. Lenders commonly assess your ability to repay loans utilizing the Affordability Approach, as they already know how much you need from your loan request. They use your financial statements to estimate whether your request should be approved. You have the choice of using either method.

If you have already determined the need for a loan and the amount you need, it is logical to utilize the Need Approach. Estimate your expected debt payment per year, assuming a certain interest rate. If the loan will not require recurring principal payments (line of credit, construction line), estimate annual interest payments only. The interest will be charged on a certain average dollar amount that you expect to be outstanding. Lenders often take a conservative approach, assuming that the lines of credit will be fully drawn all year; at the very least lenders' assumptions will be more conservative than yours. If you are requesting a term loan or a mortgage, assume a conservative repayment schedule; conservative means shorter rather than longer timeframe. Equipment is typically financed up to five to seven years, which excludes specialty, long-lasting equipment that can be financed over a longer period of time; office equipment is often financed over three years or less. Commercial mortgages are traditionally financed (or amortized) over 20 to 25 years.[1] Total your new loan debt payments and then add them to your existing payments, if any, unless your new loan request is for the purposes of refinancing old debt. Now you know your anticipated monthly or annual debt payments.

The next step is to analyze your business' operating cash flow. If your company is an established business and has been in operation for one or more years, calculate your operating cash flow and historical debt payments as shown in Appendix 5 and explained in Chapter 9. Does it appear that your business' "operating cash flow after financing" is greater than its "total debt service"? You should know that lenders often look to see if your operating cash flow after financing covers your total debt service by at least 1.2 or 1.25 times. To find that out, simply divide your operating cash flow after financing in a given year by that year's total debt service. The resulting number is what lenders call "debt service coverage". This ratio shows how many times your business' operating cash flow after financing can cover its debt payments. The higher the number, the better, because it indicates that there is a larger cushion in case your business' operating cash flow declines.

Since many small businesses generate a modest operating cash flow after financing, it is equally important to take at look at your business' ability to cover debt payment in dollar terms. Say that one year your company's debt service coverage is 1.33 times. Looks pretty good, doesn't it? But what if your company's operating cash flow after financing was $20,000 and its annual debt payment obligations were $15,000? Then the cushion is only $5,000, which is quite thin. You know better than I do that profit can decline by $5,000 quickly. In a case like this, lending officers will focus more on the dollar amount of the cash flow cushion.

Lenders will first of all review your company's historical cash flow and its ability to cover debt payments based on the recent year's financial results. You may say that next year's operating cash flow after financing will most likely be different. You might be right; however, lenders evaluate your ability to make existing plus requested debt payments on the basis of your historical cash flow and recent financial results. The best-case scenario is of course when the most recent year's operating cash flow after financing covers your company's existing and future proposed debt payments; however, this is not often the case with small businesses seeking loans.

Here is what you should do if your company's recent financial performance indicates that it may not be able to meet expected debt payments:

- Estimate whether the new, typically increased debt payments are something your company's cash flow can support. Also think about what might happen if you are able to secure loans and fail to make payments.
- If you have determined that your company cannot meet the new debt payments, you can take the following steps to persuade your lender that your business should be granted a loan:

    a) Prepare conservative and reasonable projections demonstrating that your future cash flow is likely to meet the proposed debt service. In general, your projections should not differ drastically from your recent financial performance, as it will be harder to justify them.
    b) Evaluate your historic cash flow. If you believe that you can improve your revenue or better manage your expenses, incorporate your plan of action into your projections and demonstrate how you can improve your business' cash flow.
    c) Offer other mitigating factors that are not connected with the cash flow. For instance, offer your personal guarantee, if you have substantial personal assets. Find additional collateral and, if possible, even cash collateral to strengthen your case. Think about bringing in additional guarantors.
    d) Consider other qualitative factors that could support your request. They might include your own, or one of your key manager's, experience in the field and track-record of achievements. A reasonable promise of sizeable deposits and the use of other income-generating products can make your business attractive to lenders. Also think about an SBA guarantee or some other outside support that could mitigate signs of weak cash flow or collateral or both.

Finally, let us take a brief look at the Affordability Approach. If you know that you will need some debt financing but are not sure how much you should request, calculate your historical operating cash flow after financing, as previously discussed. Note that this approach is more complicated because it requires plugging in numbers until you can estimate the amount you are able to secure. If you are mathematically inclined, plug-ins can be avoided by creating a mathematical model to do the calculations for you. When you calculate operating cash flow after financing, divide it by 1.2, which is a typical debt service coverage requirement expected by lenders. The amount you get is what you can use to make loan payments. Subtract your existing debt payment requirements from this amount. If you have something left, this is the amount in new annual debt payments you should be able to afford. Let's call this number "operating cash flow available for new loans".

Here is how you can estimate how much new debt a lender could qualify you for. If you are requesting a line of credit, assume a certain interest rate (e.g. 8%). Divide your operating cash flow available for new loans (e.g. $30,000) by 8% or .08, and you will get a line of credit of $375,000 your company can potentially qualify for. These calculations assume that the entire line is drawn all year. This is a reasonable assumption that an average lender will approve a line of credit request for $375,000 based on your company's cash flow. You may now work backward to test our calculations; divide operating cash flow after financing by the sum of the existing and new debt service requirement. You will confirm that your company can meet its debt service coverage requirement of 1.2.[2]

If you are requesting a term loan, assume the period of time you are likely to be granted the loan for (e.g. five years for many types of equipment). Multiply $30,000 by 5 (years) and you will have a term loan of $150,000. However, do not forget about interest payments, which will be highest in the first year for which we are making estimates. As a result, the term loan you can apply for will be under $150,000 and it will take you a few tries to calculate the exact amount using plug-ins.

Another way around this problem is to use a financial calculator. Most term loan payments consist of a fixed amount of principal plus interest on the outstanding amount, which means that the total monthly or annual payments fluctuate. When you know that you have only $30,000 available for annual loan payments and know the approximate loan term and interest rate, you can presume that your payments are mortgage style, which means fixed total annual payments. Using this approach, you will arrive at the total loan amount with the help of a financial calculator. As you can see, estimating the amount of debt your company can support does not have to be an exact science. You only need a ballpark figure before you begin talking with lenders.

A word of caution: you must understand that each lender reviews loan requests differently. The methodologies above may differ from lender to lender and are provided here to offer you a framework on how to improve your chances of loan approval. If you do not have any extra cash flow, then you will have to pursue a different route. If you have determined that certain actions can be taken to improve your business' cash flow in the next 12 months, prepare projections to reflect that and calculate your operating cash flow. For example, you may be able to lower owners' distributions, operating expenses, or grow your revenue. Other loan enhancing approaches will be discussed later in this book. Taking steps to analyze your company's cash flow and other factors related to loan requests will in most cases improve your chances of securing loans.

---

[1] Many websites provide mortgage and term loan calculators at no additional charge, if you do not know how to calculate annual or monthly payments yourself. See Chapter 7 for a definition of the term "amortization".
[2] Note that these calculations assume that the interest rate on your loan does not fluctuate. The example is provided for demonstration purposes only.

Chapter 11 – Does Your Financing Request Make Sense?

I have always been curious about the number of small business owners who asked themselves if their loan financing requests made sense prior to submitting them. Based on my experience in lending to small businesses, I think that a good number of them never did. You, the small business owner, periodically look at whether the prices and terms your suppliers offer you make sense and whether your customers are happy with your products, services, and prices (at least I hope you do, to ensure the financial success of your enterprises). So why not assess the basic qualities of your loan request prior to applying, if there are clear benefits to you? Here are some of the key benefits:

- You can avoid an unnecessary amount of time wasted in applying for loans
- You can improve your chances of getting your loan requests approved
- You can build credibility with prospective lenders
- You can secure better pricing and terms for your loans

Based on the information provided in the last three chapters, can you determine that your company exhibits clear signs of weak cash flow (primarily in the most recent year or in your projected cash flow)? If this is the case, focus your efforts on demonstrating how your business can improve its cash flow. For instance, provide evidence that you can reduce your compensation and distributions, you can improve revenue, you have taken steps to reduce expenses, and other steps to improve your company's cash flow, which will be paying the lenders' loans. Do not forget that promises have to be fulfilled, and failing to do so may result in negative outcomes for your company.

Also consider whether the loan amount you are requesting is more than your business can afford to pay. The problem may lie in a lack of owners' capital and taking on too much debt may put your business in jeopardy. If your business experienced some unusual negative events in the last year or two, while its cash flow in previous years was good, showing that the situation has been resolved and that the business has returned to profitability may mitigate the bad year or two. Unusual events may include a principal's attention being diverted to a family matter or to another business; a lawsuit, or the less than amicable departure of one of the owners. You do need to provide convincing evidence that the problems have been resolved. For instance, your interim financial statements might show improvement as compared to the same period last year.

Can you explain any sizeable deteriorations in your income statement or balance sheet? Make sure that you find answers prior to meeting with lenders. You are not expected to have a finance degree. However, your accountant, CFO, or even a bookkeeper should provide the necessary support to help you prepare for meetings with prospective lenders. Develop a game plan for how you can mitigate your company's financial weaknesses. It might range from actions you can take to improve the situation to bringing in the right people to address problems. The worst thing is to give lenders the impression that you are unable to do anything or did not even try to resolve problems.

Another issue that often arises is when a business requests a loan for a purpose that does not match the loan term (see the definition in Chapter 7). If you need to finance a short-term cash need that will be repaid within a year, you should do it with lines of credit, time notes, and other short-term loans. If you need to finance the acquisition of equipment or buildings, renovations, or start-up capital, you should use term, mortgage, or other types of loans used for long-term financing. Financing your various needs with the proper types of loans are basic financial management concepts and lenders will appreciate your understanding of fundamentals.

If you are using projection as the key financial statement in applying for loans, ensure that your calculations are correct and substantiated. Nothing can diminish your chances for approval more than flawed assumptions or calculations. When providing your personal guarantee to strengthen your case, make sure that you take a look at your personal credit report and score as well as your personal cash flow. If your credit report shows derogatory information and/or if your personal cash flow is negative (calculated as income minus taxes, personal debt payments, and household and living expenses), your personal guarantee may not add any weight to your business loan request – it may even hurt it.

Your loan request should stem from a financing need that was evaluated in the context of your long-term business plans. If you are requesting a loan to finance something that may contradict your vision for your company, you should ask yourself if your loan request is prudent. For instance, if you are the owner of a small hardware store and are requesting a loan to purchase a small warehouse, a lender may ask why you need it. If you have no plans for expanding your store, do not own vehicles to move inventory from or to the store, and have adequate space to store inventory in the existing store, this may be an unnecessary investment for your company and will cause a lender to doubt that are requesting a loan for the right reasons.

Last but not least, I would like to reiterate that you must have the purpose of the loan, loan amount, term, and how you are planning to repay the loan outlined at the top of your loan request.

PREPARING A LOAN REQUEST
(NON-CASH FLOW FACTORS)

There is more to loans than the cash flow and other financial data of prospective borrowers. Lenders also look at other aspects related to your business and to you personally, which will be covered in this section. If your business' cash flow is strong and ample to cover the expected debt payments, lenders are likely to lend you money even with weaknesses in collateral and personal guarantees. As this is often not the case with small businesses, knowledge of how collateral, personal guarantees, and other factors affect your chances of obtaining a loan is a must.

Chapter 12 – Collateral

The overwhelming majority of small business loans extended by the banks I have worked for required collateral (see Chapter 7 for the definition). The only instances I can recall when collateral was waived involved loans that were guaranteed by people of significant wealth and liquidity (cash, stocks, bonds, etc.) and loans to businesses that were exceptionally strong financially. In addition, the banks typically knew these individuals as customers for long periods of time. Lenders are risk-averse and need to ensure that should anything go wrong, they can go after some assets. This certainly won't be your business' cash flow, because in times of trouble the first thing your business is likely to lack is cash.

When lending to small businesses, lenders like to take a so-called lien on all of a business' assets. This includes anything your company may legally own. Business assets may include cash and investments (e.g. stock or bonds), inventory, accounts receivable, and fixed assets that encompass buildings and land, equipment, furniture and fixtures, vehicles, and software. These assets are what lenders refer to as tangible assets, which means assets that are physical, can be seen or touched, can be accounted for, taken into possession, and sold for a certain sum of money even if your company is out of business. Lenders like to see tangible assets that can potentially be sold[1] to repay loans. Another group of assets is called intangible assets. These are more elusive assets that are not likely to yield any value if repossessed and sold. They may include receivables from a company's owners or other related parties, goodwill, prepaid expenses, leasehold improvements, and other assets that are more accounting entries on paper than anything else.

Lenders typically conduct a so-called back-of-the-envelope analysis of how much they are likely to receive if your business assets were to be sold. This is a very simple assessment that involves a minimal amount of math. Each of your tangible assets is discounted by some generally acceptable percentage. For example, accounts receivable are typically discounted by 20% to 30% (sometimes more for certain types of receivables) and only receivables that are fewer than 90 days old are usually included in the calculation.[2] Inventory is traditionally discounted by 50% to 80% and some types of inventory are not eligible (e.g. perishable goods, relatively old computer or electronic parts). Once each type of asset is discounted to what lenders think they could get if they were to sell them, they add up those remaining asset values. The resulting number is compared to the sum of all loans you are expected to have, if the requested loans are approved; total discounted assets are divided by total expected loans. The resulting ratio is called the collateral coverage ratio and lenders like to see it at 1.2 or higher.

Each lender's goal is to be ahead of other lenders in case your company defaults on loan payments and its assets are liquidated. Liquidation priority is traditionally established by filing papers with the Secretary of State in the state that is home to your company. If several lending institutions have equal rights in case of liquidation, then they calculate collateral coverage by adding everyone's loans and dividing the total discounted collateral by the resulting number. If there is not enough collateral for all of them, lenders are likely to ask you for some additional collateral or your company may not get new loans. If you personally lent some money to your business, it is also very common for lenders to require that you sign a subordination agreement, which will often limit your ability to take principal and interest until your company has repaid the loans to those lenders.

Remember that there is an endless range of possibilities and approaches to calculating collateral coverage ratio. Lenders can be flexible whenever possible. However, they tend to use generally accepted industry practices because lenders are creatures of habit and experience. In the instances of lending to small businesses, lenders conduct a simple evaluation of your collateral. However, there is a type of loan arrangement called asset-based lending that is more rigorous than the process described above. You are likely to encounter it when your loans typically approach $.5 million and more in aggregate. This is when lenders lend against some specific asset, such as accounts receivable or inventory, and constantly monitor your borrowing and the levels of those assets. This type of loan requires regular financial reports such as borrowing base certificates, accounts receivable reports (receivable aging reports), or inventory listings. The frequency of those reports may vary from quarterly to monthly or even weekly. You are likely to be introduced to these loans when your company is growing in size, frequently when in the process of becoming a multi-million dollar company, but is tight on cash. Small business lenders typically do not offer asset-based arrangements as they are very labor intensive.

Lastly, what do you do when your business assets offer little to no collateral? The very next thing lenders look at is your personal assets, such as your home, investment real estate properties, and personal (non-retirement) investments. This is the point when you may have to have a difficult conversation with your spouse, as you may be putting up some of your most valuable assets as collateral. If your business fails, you risk leaving your family with nothing. Read more on personal guarantees in the next chapter. Alternatively, lenders may use the assistance of the Small Business Administration (SBA), which can guarantee up to 75% of a lender's loan, making your lender's job easier. Lenders may apply for an SBA guarantee directly or share the loan with another lending institution that specializes in SBA-guaranteed loans (e.g. SBDCs or small business development corporations throughout the United States).

Remember that when it comes to small business loans, a lender's first choice is satisfactory cash flow. Satisfactory collateral is not there to replace a lack of cash flow. It is there to provide additional comfort, but may be used to mitigate some cash flow weaknesses. However, it is not a solution to bad cash flow.[3]

---

[1] Note that even tangible assets may not have much value. This includes obsolete or damaged inventory, damaged or otherwise useless equipment, accounts receivable for work yet to be completed, and many others.
[2] The formulas vary from one lending institution to another. Some lenders have strict formulas while others use their experience and best judgment.
[3] One of few exceptions to the rule I experienced in my lending career was the use of cash and marketable securities as collateral for securing a loan.

Chapter 13 - Personal Guarantee

A personal guarantee is a promise by an individual involved in and benefiting from the business to repay the loan if the company goes into default and is unable to make payments.[1] There are other guarantees, such as corporate (guarantee by another company), but they are beyond the scope of our discussion. A personal guarantee for small business loans is almost always a must, because the financial performance of small companies may fluctuate significantly. In addition, when a company is commonly owned by only one individual or a family, lenders want to be able to have those individuals on the hook, should anything go wrong with the loan repayment. The key reasons why lenders ask for personal guarantees are to have a psychological effect on the guarantor (constant reminder), to give lenders access to the guarantor's personal assets, and to help in enforcing loan repayment through the court system.

Note that a personal guarantee is typically not a secured promise, meaning you are not securing the loan with specific personal assets. When you pledge specific assets, lenders would first go after those assets and those assets only, as it is easier to reach them legally.[1] With a personal guarantee, which is also known as an unsecured guarantee, it is not as easy for lenders to go after personal property as it is with a secured promise. However, rest assured that lenders will likely do whatever they can within the legal limits to get their money back. The most common example is a lender placing an attachment or lien on a guarantor's personal residence; the lender takes place after the existing mortgage lender(s) and taps into the equity the guarantor has in the house.

A personal guarantee may be limited or unlimited. During my small business lending career I encountered unlimited guarantees most frequently. This means that you are guaranteeing any debt incurred by a given small business, which may include any future debt, unless the guarantee agreement limits your guarantee to the existing business debt only. In addition, you may be liable for related legal fees, default interest payments and related assessments – in common terms, you are obligated to make good on everything related to the company's loan should something go wrong.[2] Limited guarantee limits your liability only to a particular loan or dollar amount and nothing else. The loan agreement should spell out explicitly what you are responsible for. While limited liability is more beneficial for a guarantor, lenders may not be inclined to let you get away with a limited promise.

I would also like to mention the consideration issue related to personal guarantees. In the past several years, some regulators and the legal counsels of some lending institutions have been outspoken in advising lenders on who is able to guarantee a company's debt. It is now a requirement for some lenders that there be a so-called consideration, which means that the guarantor must derive some direct or indirect benefit from the company and therefore the loan.[3] This step was taken to move away from what historically were guarantees by people who are not even involved in the business, such as friends, relatives, and unrelated parties. Those individuals may not even know what is going on with the company and derive no direct or indirect benefit from the loan. Therefore, it is not just to make them responsible for someone else's debt, and courts have historically frowned upon and refused to enforce such guarantees.

When it comes to obtaining the loan your company needs, it is not the guarantee that matters but its quality. The quality of your personal guarantee is commonly determined by analyzing your personal assets, personal income, and personal credit history. Personal credit history and credit score have been in the spotlight in the past ten years and deserve a separate discussion in the following chapter.

To analyze your personal assets, you will be asked to fill out a personal financial statement, or PFS. A PFS can contain several pages and consists of a balance sheet, a statement of income and expenses, various schedules, questionnaires, and disclosures that state your responsibilities and rights. PFS contain language that allows lenders to obtain your personal credit reports. Lending officers typically use PFS to procure information about your personal assets: liquid assets (cash, CDs, stocks, bonds, and other similar assets that can be easily converted to cash), real estate holdings (residence and investment real estate), cash surrender value of life insurance (if any), retirement investments, and net worth (your personal assets minus personal debt). Other assets such as personal belongings, autos, receivables from other individuals or entities, and the value of your business do not usually deserve credit or consideration.

While PFS contain the income statement, lending officers typically analyze your income by obtaining your personal tax returns. However, information in the PFS can be cross-referenced and compared in a search for possible fraud. Lenders look to calculate your income after taxes. They then subtract your various living expenses and annual debt payments to determine if there is any cash left afterwards. If there is an excess, loan officers can make a justification that some of this extra cash could be put back into the company, which means that you could potentially lower your compensation and strengthen your business cash flow. Lenders also calculate your debt-to-income ratio, which is calculated as monthly or annual debt payments divided by gross income for the same period. If the ratio falls somewhere between 34% and 40% or higher, for most lenders it would mean that you have too much debt and are pushing the limits. The lower this number is, the better.

The stronger your personal guarantee, the more likely it is to enhance your business loan request and mitigate weaknesses in your business cash flow or collateral.

---

[1] Note that lenders may be able to go after your other assets if, in addition to securing a loan with specific personal asset, you also provide an unlimited or limited personal guarantee that may allow lenders to go after your other personal property. Be watchful of the forms you sign!

[2] Note that non-payment is one of many other reasons that can trigger a default (please check your loan agreement). Instances of default may include a change of ownership or the sale of the business without the lender's prior approval, or obtaining loans from another lender without the original lender's prior approval.

[3] Based on my discussions with lenders in various parts of the country, this practice may vary from one region to another and from one lender to another. As far as I am aware, this is not yet a federally-required practice.

Chapter 14 – Personal Credit History

As mentioned previously, small business lenders frequently look to owners to guarantee business loans. Based on my experience in banking, your personal credit history is one of the first pieces of information lenders investigate when evaluating the quality of your personal guarantee. Your credit history serves as a predictor of your future behavior with regard to your personal loans and, indirectly, to business loans you may be asked to guarantee. Credit history investigations can be formal or informal (the author's terms). A formal history is gathered and mathematically evaluated by the credit reporting agencies, while an informal history relates to credit references you can provide yourself.

A formal credit history is collected by the three main credit reporting agencies or credit bureaus: Experian, Equifax, and Transunion. Imagine the entire industry that developed around gathering, grading, and selling information about how you, the consumer, pay your bills and manage your credit. The credit bureaus collect information about your credit history (lender or creditor information, type of loan, balance, monthly payments, and payment history), which includes public information such as tax liens and bankruptcies. In addition, they gather your personal information such as current and past addresses, social security number, date of birth as well as inquiries about your credit rating by third parties. All this data is collected for one single purpose – to calculate your final credit score.

One of the most widespread mathematical models to calculate your score was developed by Fair Isaac, now a publicly traded company. As a result, the score is often referred to as the FICO score. The model that calculates your score focuses 75% on payment history and the amounts you owe.[1] Less influential factors consist of length of credit history, new credit information, and types of credit used. The goal of the credit scoring model is to assess the likelihood of your becoming delinquent for 90 days on any of your consumer loans within next two years.[2]

The FICO score ranges from 300 to 850, although each individual credit reporting agency may have a slightly different range. There is truly no such thing as the right score, but the higher your score, the better. To give you some guidelines, at the time this was being written, www.myfico.com was reporting a median FICO score in the U.S. of 723. In addition, www.experian.com reported an average national score index of 677. Fifty-eight percent of the U.S. population have FICO scores of 700 and above.[1] Each credit reporting agency may have a somewhat different score for each individual, because it may not have the exact same information the other agencies do.

There is no precise minimum score. First of all, lenders use different tools to approve small business loans. A score of 700 may be excellent for one lender, while only a passing minimum for another. In addition, different lenders may use different credit agencies, and some may use credit reports that combine scores from all three credit bureaus. Based on my experience, scores in the high 600s and above are typically considered satisfactory, while scores in low 600s and below may raise questions, concerns, or even result in declined loan requests. The poor quality of your personal credit record means that your personal guarantee may offer little value to lenders and may cost your company its business loan.

It is important to remember that focusing too much on your credit score may lead to obsession. Think of it as a reflection of how you handle your credit. Pay your bills on time, work to reduce your debt, do not use credit cards as your only financing tool, keep your personal information secure, prevent identity theft, and periodically check your credit reports for accuracy, particularly as some states have passed laws enabling you to receive free credit report(s) each year. If you do all that, your credit score will likely be satisfactory.

An informal credit history is my term for your credit references. They can be a powerful tool to enhance your credit history picture. While lenders ask you to provide information on institutions and individuals who can give you credit references, in my experience lenders do not always check that information. However, you may consider providing letters of reference from your existing banks and other financial institutions as long as they are credible. I suggest avoiding references from family members and friends, as they are not usually considered objective. Informal credit references can be valuable in situations when you lack a formal credit history (if you are new to this country or have not borrowed in past years) or your history and credit score are somewhat below average.

Remember that while your credit history does not always predict how you will act in the future, particularly in life-changing circumstances, it has proven to be a reliable tool in evaluating your qualities as a guarantor of small business loans. From credit information about you, prospective lenders try to assess your integrity, responsibility, honesty, and respect for the credit system.

---

[1] Information taken from www.myfico.com, credit education tab. Credit reporting agencies also have credit explanation and education sections on their websites: www.experian.com, www.equifax.com and www.transunion.com.
[2] "The Role of Credit Scores in Consumer Lending Today", Elizabeth Mays, October 2003, RMA Journal.

Chapter 15 – Quality of Your Management Team

While I have gained considerable experience in the financial service sector and have a good working knowledge of finance, like thousands of lenders I did not have an appreciation and understanding of what it meant to be a small business owner before I began to take my first steps in establishing my own small business. Small business ownership, as you know, means being a jack of all trades. It is impractical and often impossible to have a thorough knowledge of all areas of business operation: trade, management, finance, and marketing. The key quality of a small business owner is the ability to manage a successful business with limited knowledge, to quickly learn only what you need to know to run your business, and to use other people's expertise to help you fill in knowledge gaps.

Many small business owners I have had an opportunity to work with were proficient in their trade and viewed that as the most important skill. However, lenders do not share this sentiment and are certain that it is the management skills of the owner that determine whether a small business will successfully repay loans. I tend to agree with their reasoning. Knowledge of your trade allows you to potentially create a superior product or service, but does not usually help you in delivering it to your customer or in getting paid.

For instance, if you are the owner of an ice cream shop, such as the founders of Ben and Jerry's Ice Cream, you know how to make the famous Chunky Monkey and Cherry Garcia ice creams (my apologies to those of you who prefer other brands). However, to manage and grow a profitable ice cream shop you need to raise the funding to buy equipment, have cash to purchase supplies and rent a location, manage incoming cash, coordinate the actions of various suppliers, train and monitor the behavior of a couple of employees, promote your products, and a multitude of other tasks. Knowledge of how to make ice cream alone will not help make that happen. It is good management expertise that helps you bring various pieces of your business puzzle together, keeps your company under control, and manages the stresses of daily tasks. As a result, good management skills are what leads your company to profitability, help it meet projections, and serve as an assurance for lenders that you will repay loans.

Lenders prefer that you have at least some basic financial knowledge, although it is not a must. The knowledge gap can be filled by having an employee or an outside party (e.g. an accountant) who can provide you with quality advice and service in that area. What lenders do like to see is good book-keeping practices, an understanding of your company's cash flow, and restraint on the use of debt financing. The proof that you possess good management skills can be manifested in the past successes of your company and its profitable performance, in management experiences before you became a small business owner, and other examples that can demonstrate a track record of accomplishment. Last but not least, it is invaluable for every owner of a small business to continue improving his of her management skills, particularly in the area of organizing, managing, and motivating employees to keep the business profitable. Lack of management skills can be a strong deterrent in approving a loan request, if your business also lacks satisfactory cash flow and collateral.

CHAPTER 16 – BUSINESS CREDIT HISTORY

In addition to looking at the personal credit history of the guarantors, lenders also check your business' credit history. A business credit history typically includes the timeliness of payments to your past creditors (e.g. lenders, suppliers); public records (e.g. tax liens, legal judgments, and bankruptcies); and liens on your business assets. As small business companies are frequently owned by an individual, a family, or a small group of private owners, lenders believe that the likelihood of credit repayment is driven by the habit of its owners and does not change overnight. Thus, a business credit history is used to predict with some degree of certainty how your company will treat the debt of its prospective lenders. A business credit history can be formal or informal (the author's terms).

A formal credit history is investigated differently by different lenders. Some do not even use formal approaches at all due to high costs. In my banking career I came across two major sources of formal credit checks: Dun and Bradstreet (or D&B) and Experian Intelliscore reports. I sometimes find these sources useful in obtaining information on payment experience to suppliers and other creditors, lien filings, and public records. However, this information is frequently outdated and lenders in many instances have a more complete picture of your company than D&B or Experian. One of the key reasons for the lack of up-to-date information is protectiveness of small business owners. Small business owners do not see the incentive for disclosing their business information when contacted by business credit agencies. In theory, incorrect and outdated information may potentially have a negative impact on your company's rating and its chances of securing loans. However, lenders do not rely solely on those reports and it is your choice whether you want to volunteer information about your companies to D&B, Experian, and others. At this point, business credit reports are not the powerful and widespread tools that personal credit reports are, but they do have a certain value for lenders who are willing to accept the costs.

Informal business credit references are also valuable in the world of small business lending. There is a multitude of businesses and individuals who can potentially give you a credit reference. This includes your existing lenders and other creditors, deposit institutions (most often banks), accountants, lawyers, suppliers, former and existing business partners, landlords, and anybody with whom you have had financial and business transactions. When selecting someone to ask for a reference, make sure that an individual or an organization is prepared to vouch for your company. The quality of any company is determined by the people who represent it, from owners and to entry-level employees. While some of your references haven't lent you money, they can attest to your company's integrity, trustworthiness, and business ethic. Last but not least, lenders may conduct their own independent investigations, which include speaking with experts in your industries, competitors, or even customers, particularly if lenders have a business relationship with those individuals or companies.

Chapter 17 – The Five Cs of Credit and Why You Need to Know Them

The Five Cs of credit are the most fundamental concepts in business lending. They can give you good insights into what lenders focus on. They echo back to everything discussed so far in this book and underscore the fact that securing small business loans can be a predictable and manageable process for small business entrepreneurs. Here are the five Cs of credit: Character, Capacity, Capital, Collateral, and Conditions.[1]

Character refers to the quality of senior managers, who are the same as owners in most small businesses. Character is evaluated in the context of making good on the promise to repay debt. It is usually defined in terms of integrity, honesty, trustworthiness, and diligence. Even if you have never borrowed from or banked with a particular financial institution, there is often evidence of how you handled yourself with other lenders, customers, suppliers, and business associates. References or personal credit reports can provide some degree of insight into your character. Character has nothing to do with your level of expertise in the industry or your intelligence. It is a quality you have, and the proof of it is typically built over years. For instance, one of my former business customers had serious health problems and experienced family turmoil but, with the help of his business associates, always ensured that his company's debt obligations were paid on time. It is never too early to begin building your reputation.

Capacity refers to your business' ability to make loan payments. This quality concerns your business cash flow. Unlike character, capacity can be assessed quantitatively based on your company's historical financial data and projections. You can use the method described in the book to estimate your company's ability to service the existing and new debt the way lenders do it. Some businesses have a strong cash flow, some insufficient, but the majority of small businesses will probably fall somewhere in between, or have a tight cash flow. Among the immediate ways to improve your business' cash flow is by understanding and reducing expenses and increasing prices whenever possible. However, a predictable and satisfactory cash flow is built over a long period of time.

Capital refers to the combination of owners' equity and debt that finances your company's assets. There are many ways in which you can evaluate whether your company has the right mix of debt versus equity, some of which can be very technical and complicated. I suggest keeping it simple. Is your cash flow too tight to support existing debt payments, or is it expected to be tight if the requested loans are approved? If that is the case, your equity may be inadequate for the level of cash flow your business produces. Furthermore, refer to the industry statistics and compare your company's capital structure (amount of equity versus debt) to that of your competitors. If your company's relationship between debt and equity is substantially different from that of your competition, perhaps you can improve the way you finance your assets. The anecdotal standard is that a business should have at least 20%-30% in equity and the rest in debt, but there is really no such thing as the right amount of equity. The goal is to maximize profits with the least amount of equity possible.

Collateral refers to the business assets you are willing and able to pledge to support your loan request, in case your company defaults on debt payments and the lender needs to sell the collateral to get repaid. While there is no precise way to determine whether your assets amount to sufficient collateral, this quality can be evaluated quantitatively. Determine whether your asset is tangible or intangible, as discussed in Chapter 12. Lenders are much less inclined to lend to small businesses against intangible assets, unless their value can be reliably established and they can be sold. If your company's cash flow is very strong, lenders are more likely to accept weaker collateral. They are much less inclined to do the same for companies with poor cash flow but very strong collateral, unless this collateral is in cash or marketable securities (bonds, stocks, etc.).

Conditions refer to your industry and economic conditions, which are qualitative in nature and are not as easy to evaluate as cash flow or collateral. Evaluating possible conditions risks has been compared to shaking a box (the box is your loan request) and comparing it to previous boxes.[2] There is no guarantee that all risks can be accounted for or assessed correctly. This category tries to assess how vulnerable or sensitive your business is to what is happening or likely to happen with your industry in a given economic environment. There are always some significant risks that can ruin your company. Your goal is to address those risks ahead of time, as it is not only important for lenders, but is also important for the very survival of your company. For many small businesses the arrival of new competitors in the immediate area, changes in the disposable income of consumers, a significant increase in supplier prices, or the loss of a major customer can have devastating effects. While it is almost impossible to completely shelter your company from these risks, lenders can evaluate whether your company's time in business and reputation, quality of its products or services, price, current customer base, and other qualities adequately mitigate conditions risks.

The use of these concepts is almost second nature for lenders, and is something we learn in one of our first lending classes. Your job is to identify whether any of the Cs are weaknesses in your case, to find ways to reduce and therefore mitigate them, and to develop a longer-term strategy on how to improve. If you analyze the above Cs and try to address questions and concerns that might arise from your prospective lenders, you will considerably improve your chances of obtaining loans and make your business stand out from other small businesses that are not aware of the five Cs.

---

[1] Note that there may be varying interpretations of the Cs and their definitions in the lending community.
[2] "Bankers, Betas, and the Cs of Credit", article by William H. Lepley in December 03 / January 04 RMA Journal.

PUTTING ALL THE INFORMATION TOGETHER

By now you should have an understanding of your company's financial situation, its cash flow, the amount you need to borrow, the various factors that go into the loan approval, and the strengths and weaknesses of your loan request. This section will help you shape the information you have into a Request for Loan Proposal or RLP.

Chapter 18 – Organizing Your Information

Small business owners often ask me if they should create a business plan or some other document to summarize their loan requests and their companies' qualities. Considering that the size of your loan request is likely to be under $1 million and in many instances even less than $100,000, a business plan in its traditional sense will probably be excessive. This does not, however, mean that going through the exercise of creating a business plan is a waste of time. It is simply not required in applying for most small business loans.[1]

As small business owners typically apply for loans with several lenders, there is a good chance that at least some of those lenders will be community-based, smaller-sized banks. Smaller banks tend to spend more time analyzing your company's financial statements and their particular conditions, and creating an RLP will have its benefits. See Chapter 25 for more information on the benefits and the shortcomings of applying for loans with smaller and larger lenders. If you are certain that you will only apply with one or more large lenders that utilize an automated or scored approval programs, then you should only use a short RLP, the primary goal of which is organizing your thoughts.

The only way for you to find out if your prospective lender uses a scoring method to review small business loan requests is to ask. I presume that by now you already know the loan amount you will be applying for, without which lenders will not be able to tell you whether your loan will be scored (bear in mind that large lenders score loans only up to certain dollar amount). If your loan will be scored, all you usually need to do is gather your business and personal financial statements and have them available.

The goal of the RLP is to summarize information about your loan request, the most important and pertinent information about your business, show how you mitigate key risks, and summarize your company's financial data. The length of this document should be 3 to 5 pages of text and attachments with financial information. Being concise and focusing only on applicable information is the key to creating a successful RLP. In essence, it is a mini-business plan to support your loan request. Brevity will help you save time for yourself and allow your prospective lenders to learn about your business in about an hour. Below is a possible outline for your Request for Loan Proposal.

Full Request for Loan Proposal[2]

- Executive Summary – 1 to 2 paragraphs
    Loan purpose, amount, requested loan term, the nature of your company's business, its strengths, ownership, management's experience and key qualifications, business goals for the next 2-3 years and how they will be achieved, competition and why customers choose your company over competitors.
- Company background – 1 paragraph, up to ½ page
    Nature of business, time in business, history, key business strengths, achievements, number of employees and their key skills.
- Ownership and management team – 1 paragraph
    Names, ownership details, key management figures and responsibilities, their skills, qualifications, and achievements.
- Industry background – 1 to 2 paragraphs
    Industry background and dynamics, recent trends, how they affect your company, what it takes to succeed in your industry.
- Competition and your marketing plan – ½ to 1 page
    Your key competitors, their strengths and weaknesses, how your business is different or similar, how your business strategy has allowed and will continue to allow you to compete successfully, and why customers choose your products and services. Outline the key goals and strategies in your marketing plan.
- Overview of your company's financial performance for the last 2-3 years – ½ page
    Discuss only key trends, focus on explaining negatives

or deteriorations and what you have done to improve the situation.
- Projections (if any) – ½ page discussion
- Main business risks and mitigating factors – ½ paragraph
    This section is a summary, the crown jewel of your RLP – identify the key risks your business is facing or will face in the near future and indicate what you are doing to reduce their impact.
- Attachments
    Your company's historical and projected financial statements.

Short Request for Loan Proposal[2]

Datasheet about your company in a bullet-point format:
- Loan amount, purpose, and requested loan term
- How you expect to repay

Data about your company
- Nature of business and year established
- Ownership and management outline and responsibilities
- Key services and products
- Key strengths
- Key weakness and threats as well as mitigating factors.

---

[1] A common exception to this rule is a start-up small business, but even in such cases I recommend keeping it concise.

[2] Format, template, and proposed content of the RLP are the author's copyrighted material. No reproduction is permitted without a prior written permission by the author.

Chapter 19 – Mock Interviews and Preparation for Meetings with Lenders

Proper preparation for applying for loans, including preparation for meetings with prospective lenders, is in my opinion almost as important as having adequate cash flow to repay your loans. Your prep plan should contain at least three components: preparing your financial statements, anticipating and addressing questions lenders are likely to ask, and practicing your answers to develop confidence and comfort.

Preparing your financial statements

Depending on the total amount of loans with one particular lender, you may be asked to provide tax returns or compiled, reviewed, or audited financial statements prepared by your accountant. At the very least each small business should have internal financial statements and business tax returns. It is your choice whether you want to pay for compiled, reviewed, or audited financial statements before you know what your lender is likely to require. After all, these financial statements cost money, ranging from under $1,000 to $10,000 and even more depending on the complexity of your operations. If you do want to get a sense of what financial statements may be required, contact lenders to ask some preliminary questions (see Chapter 29 for details). In my experience, many community-based banks with total loan relationships of less than $200,000-$300,000 per business allow tax returns. For large lenders this threshold is pushing $1 million.[1] The more money you borrow, the more your lender is likely to ask you to provide more sophisticated and, therefore, more expensive financial statements. If you track your accounts receivable and accounts payable, I also suggest having a recent copy of those financial statements handy.

In addition to business financial statements, I suggest gathering information about your personal assets, such as your assets and liabilities. Since in most cases small business lenders will ask for the guarantee of the owners, you will be asked to fill out personal financial statements. Gathering your personal financial information in advance will save you time when you are ready to fill out application documents. Some people's assets are quite simple and will only include checking accounts, retirement accounts, and a house. For others, it is impossible to sit down and give correct asset balances on a short notice. Also have your personal tax returns for the past 2-3 years handy. Personal financial statements frequently contain sections that outline your income and expenses, and your tax returns may come in handy. If your personal guarantee is one of the main strengths of your loan application, have a recent copy of your brokerage or bank account statements, as lenders may ask for them as a proof of your financial strength.

Anticipating and addressing questions lenders are likely to ask

To develop a rapport with and make lenders confident in your company's ability to repay the debt, you must anticipate lender's questions and concerns. While you will not be able to cover all possibilities, you can reduce the number of surprise questions. Below are several suggestions that will help you become prepared to have a conversation with lenders.

- Be prepared to discuss your business' financing needs (loan request) and your business' goals (at least a two-three year plan). You should aim to establish a link between your need for the money and your business goals. Also be prepared to talk about your overall banking needs, as lenders are trying to develop relationships, not just approve loans.
- Be prepared to discuss any visible weaknesses in your business' cash flow, potential loan collateral, and your guarantee.
- Be prepared to present your business' qualities, its strengths and weaknesses. Lenders will particularly be interested in weaknesses and will want to see that the existing strengths or your business strategy balance those weaknesses.
- Be prepared to talk about your industry's condition, how it affects your business, what challenges your company is faced with, and how you are reducing those risks.
- Be prepared to discuss your company's historical financial performance, particularly any deteriorations in revenue, profitability, cash flow, liquidity, or net worth. In addition, make

sure that you discuss what you have done to correct and improve the situation. Be as factual and as conservative as you can.
- Be prepared to discuss your personal assets and your personal cash flow. This includes any possible late payments, tax liens, judgments, tight personal cash flow, and others. Also have a summary of what you have done to improve the situation.

Practicing your answers to develop confidence and comfort

Simulating an actual meeting with lenders at least once is not a waste of time. When you run through a few possible scenarios, it should give you a greater level of confidence and comfort speaking with prospective lenders. There are various ways in which you can practice. Using the bullet points presented above, you can draft a list of possible questions. You can read them to yourself or have your business associate or a family member pose them to you. You should answer questions aloud, which will help you build confident composure, tone of voice, and comfort level.

In conclusion, I would like to emphasize that your answers should be brief and limited to three to five minutes. Keep each question in mind and focus only on answering one specific question at a time. Lenders are very busy people. Thus, do not turn your Q&A session into a lecture. As hard as it may sound, make efforts to remove passion for your business from this conversation. Lenders want to see realistic, conservative, and reasonable business people. I understand that for many small business owners their businesses are their lives. However, do not let your passion prevent you from securing the loans your business needs.

---

[1] This number is provided as a guide. Actual financial statement requirements may vary. In addition, lenders have historically been loosening their requirements.

KNOW YOUR LENDER!

From my very first credit training class as a banker, I learned a single phrase – know your customer. I believe that every small business owner must learn the phrase "know your lender", as this will help you secure the loans you seek and will help you manage your credit relationship to your liking. As a banker, I do not like surprises and always try to be prepared for the unexpected. Similarly, you should avoid surprises. Your preparation will reward you. This section will help you understand why lenders behave the way we do, how we operate, what pet peeves we have, what we expect, and what we think about you – small business owners.

CHAPTER 20 – THE BANKING ENVIRONMENT AND HOW IT BENEFITS YOU

The first thing you need to know about the present lending environment in the U.S. is: competition, competition, competition. The rising costs of complying with regulations, increasing salaries and benefits, and the constant need to invest in technology as well as stiff competition were the factors behind the decline in the number of banks from 14,628 in 1975 to 7,712 as of March 31, 2004.[1]

The lending landscape consists of a few very large financial institutions and lots of small community-based banks and lending companies. For example, only nine FDIC-insured banks hold 48% of industry assets, and 419 banks hold a total of 85% of industry assets. The most money is in the hands of very few banks, which also happen to be commercial lending companies. What does all this mean to you, the small business owner? It means that there is a lot of competition for your business loans and a lot of credit (loans) available to qualify for. In addition, non-banking financial institutions are fighting for a piece of the same pie. You just need to know how to approach them the right way. In my conversations with lenders or loan officers I hear the same ever-present theme – it is becoming more and more difficult to find new, worthy loan customers, because competitors steal them in an instant.

Lenders compete on everything from pricing to services and products. Free checking and no closing costs are becoming almost a given. Due to this incredible amount of competition, some lenders are willing to lower pricing beyond sensible levels just to make you move your relationship to them. Lenders also work on cutting the time it takes to review your loan requests and roll out new products and on-line services that are designed to help you in financing and managing your business. While some of you may argue the above points, I would like to underscore that the money is there.

---

[1] S&P Industry Studies, Banking Industry report, 8/19/04

CHAPTER 21 – WHAT LENDERS EXPECT

Lenders are traditionally very patient people. They do not want to disappoint their customers out of fear of losing their business. Unlike investors who may want 15%-20% or an even higher return for investing cash into your company, lenders are often happy with prime rate or some equivalent of that rate plus some small spread. This translates into half or less than half of what equity investors will charge you. Despite lenders' patient nature, they do have expectations that you should be aware of. Here is a short list of some key expectations.

- Lenders want to be assured that you or someone in your company has basic financial competence and understands essential concepts such as cash flow, profitability, and net worth. It is commonly accepted that a small business owner may not be proficient in various aspects of business operations. However, some financial knowledge is crucial in giving lenders the assurance that their money will be handled properly.

- Lenders want proof that you understand the inner workings of your company and the industry it operates in. This is revealed by analyzing your past achievements as a manager as well as demonstrated by the financial performance of your company.

- If you are starting a business, lenders would like to know that you have direct experience in the field in which you are planning on making profits and repaying their loans. Many people aspire to become business owners. However, some entrepreneurs venture into business without sufficient experience in a particular line of business.

- Lenders want to see you and anyone else in charge have some management experience – many people can dream but only a few can make the dream reality. For a one-person business, management skills mean good time-management and project-management skills and discipline. For businesses with employees, good management means the ability to organize and motivate people and to prioritize your time as a manager.

- Lenders want to see small business owners handle their loan relationships professionally and respectfully. I have witnessed instances when customers were unprofessional and even abusive, when they disregarded the terms of the loan agreement, ignored lenders' requests, and had no regard for the fact that lenders are also people. Lenders' and their companies' patience can run only so far. Although this does not happen often, I am aware of instances when lenders informed customers that their business was no longer welcome.

- Lenders want to see business owners who are honest and forthcoming with information that may negatively affect their company's ability to make loan repayments. When your company is in financial trouble, it usually does not go away quickly. By not communicating with lenders about your problems, you are running the risk of catching lenders by surprise, if they find out about your situation indirectly. Signs of trouble can be uncovered from a business credit report, from your customers or suppliers, or from late loan payments. If this happens, lenders may not be inclined to give you additional time to turns things around.

- Lenders expect to win your business relationship, not just a loan. Many lenders will not profit solely by extending loans to small companies. Profits come from an array of services: your deposits, credit and merchant card services, payroll processing, investments, and many others. They too need to make profits to stay in business. Consequently, it is wise to think about what you can bring to the table to make lenders value the possibility of your company's patronage.

Some of the above points are the same expectations business owners have for their business associates, customers, and suppliers. While more and more people expect certain financial services at no charge, you should realize that lenders expect to be treated in a certain way. The sooner you understand and take advantage of this knowledge, the sooner you will be on the way to securing the financing your company needs and establishing mutually rewarding relationships with your creditors.

CHAPTER 22 – LENDER'S PET PEEVES: SITUATIONS TO AVOID

From the previous chapter you know what some of the essential expectations of lenders are. It is now time to focus on what they truly dislike. Of course, dislikes may differ from one loan officer to another. However, the lending industry is quite structured, in many respects even uniform. As a result, there are typically a handful of situations you would want to avoid with almost every lender.

- **Negative financial surprises** (e.g. operating losses, cash flow problems) **that may jeopardize your company's ability to make loan and interest payments.** As lenders are risk-averse people, they hate those moments, particularly when they have just heard that your company is doing well. By the terms of the loan agreement you will be required to submit your business' financial statement at certain intervals. In addition, lenders may periodically conduct a credit check on your company. You should also note that some lending institutions, particularly the larger ones, may not have much tolerance for negative performance even when you are forthcoming with bad news. Nevertheless, my personal lending experience and interviews with lenders tell me that communicating with lenders about your company's negative financial results will get you farther than being silent about them.

- **Violations of loan agreements, frequently identified as instances of default.** This commonly includes a change in ownership or the sale of collateral without the lender's prior agreement or borrowing from another lender without prior permission. It will come as a surprise to many small business owners that they have to ask their lender's permission to bring in another partner, to buy or sell their business, or to sell what is now the lender's collateral. I can expect you to say that this is your business, and you are entitled to do what you think is best for it. Well, the moment you sign a loan agreement, you have to play by the lender's rules outlined in that contract. I strongly encourage you to review the documents you sign, particularly the covenant and default sections.

- **Use of the loan proceeds for other than their intended purposes**, such as using business loans for personal needs and pleasure or the use of a line of credit to purchase a building. When you request a loan, it is for a particular purpose. Lenders structure a repayment plan based on the loan purpose. When you use the money for something else, it means that you still need the money for that original purpose; you misused the money the lender entrusted to you, and you potentially threaten the viability of your business. The best away to avoid this situation is to be honest about the purpose of your loan and have the discipline to spend the money the way it was intended.

- **Concealing information that can be discovered during the loan request review process** such as prior bankruptcies, pending lawsuits, or ownership in other companies that may take your attention away from the business borrowing the money. Providing false information is fraud. However, there are instances when small business owners might be tempted not to volunteer potentially damaging information in hopes that lenders will not discover it. In today's age of technology, lenders have more and more tools at their disposal to look into the pasts of businesses and their owners. Data that used to be the privilege of large institutions with significant financial resources is now available to smaller lending companies. You should think twice if you want to take this chance with your prospective, or even with your existing loan relationship.

- **Dishonesty and delays in the submission of financial statements that show losses.** Some small business owners delay the submission of financial statements in hopes of postponing the discovery of bad news. What they may not realize is that significant delays and continuous excuses raise red flags for lenders. At some point a lender may become uncomfortable with the wait and refer to the loan agreement for possible actions. Not only do you ruin the good relations you have with your lender, but you may also preclude your company from getting loans in the future from the same lending institution. You also risk exposing your business to potentially damaging legal actions lenders may take. While lenders do not like losses any more than you do, being honest and showing lenders the steps you are taking to improve the situation is perhaps the only dignified and safe way out.

- **Being extremely cooperative, available, and polite when you need money and disappearing when lenders need your attention.** This is what I call the "user" mentality: I use you when I need you, and your interests are of no concern to me. I caution all small business owners about this type of behavior. While lenders may be tolerant people, particularly with their most valuable customers, all businesses go through cycles. Even strong companies are bound to hit rough spots. Do you think your lender will be out there for you when your business needs money? Loans are typically ample for businesses that do not need them. Companies have the most difficult time securing loans when they are in desperate need of them. I recommend creating goodwill with your lenders, so that when you need them they will be there for you just like you were there for them.

- **Submitting information that is not supported by your financial statements or submitting incorrect financial documents.** There are lots of examples of sloppily prepared information, inconsistencies, and pure fraud. Some of the most typical examples: 1) providing projections with profit or cash flow showing one amount and discussing this information with the help of supplementary documents that show absolutely different information; 2) financial statements with basic math that does not add up; 3) providing an altered copy of financial statements that were previously submitted. There is only one solution to this problem: verify the information you say or send to lenders. While this may sound like a time-consuming proposition, think of the lost time and money in trying to get loans and not getting them because you didn't pay attention. It is also dangerous to think that lenders do not have enough experience or intelligence to detect your lack of preparation.

In conclusion, I would like to say that it is up to you whether you choose to use this information to your advantage. The key point is that lenders are as human as small business owners. They have their likes and dislikes. Loan officers take seriously anything that may threaten loan repayment because their careers and their families' livelihoods are at stake. Lenders may lose their jobs if they grant too many bad loans. Use this information for your own benefit. Keep lenders happy, and they will work hard to take care of your business needs.

CHAPTER 23 – HELP LENDERS UNDERSTAND YOUR INDUSTRY AND MAKE THEM MORE COMFORTABLE WITH YOUR LOAN REQUEST

Your goal is to secure the loan you need, while the lender's goal is to understand your company's financial and non-financial qualities to become comfortable with giving it money. Industry analysis is important to every lender, unless perhaps your loan is secured by cash or marketable securities (stocks, bonds, etc.). One of the first things that you, the business owner, should know is that lenders have a limited amount of time to review your loan requests and make decisions. As it is impossible for lenders to know and understand every industry, you can and should help them understand the industry in which your business operates. This will help your prospective lenders develop the necessary level of comfort to improve your chances in securing loans your company needs and deserves. To achieve this goal, follow these three steps: 1) talk about key driving forces in your industry; 2) explain what risks exists for your company in the industry; and 3) demonstrate what actions you have taken to mitigate main industry risks to help your company succeed.

1. Talk about key driving forces in your industry

There is no such thing as industry without risks. Every company faces a variety of problems and challenges on a daily basis ranging from the arrival of new competitors to the loss of customers as a result of a decrease in disposable income. When a lender reviews a loan request from a company in an unfamiliar industry, for example a martial arts business, the lack of industry knowledge and understanding can make the lender skeptical and cautious about granting the loan. Loan decision-making is almost like a two-column table with pluses on the one side and minuses on the other. If the minuses outweigh the pluses, your business is out of luck and you will have to continue looking for financing. Do not lose points on something as simple as not sharing with your prospective loan officer information about your industry.

Each lending institution, whether it is a bank or a financing company, avoids extending loans to those customers who operate in risky industries. Larger financial institutions have lists of industries that are called prohibited industries (cannot lend to companies in those industries under any circumstances) and non-preferred industries (do not lend unless there is something special about that company or loan request). Smaller community banks are less formal and simply cautious about lending to certain industries, these commonly include restaurants, construction contractors, gas stations, high tech companies, and some others. It does not hurt to ask a loan officer if his or her institution lends to companies in your industry.

2. Explain what risks your business faces in the industry

Talk about your industry's most important issues, including risks, and how they impact your enterprise. The risks may include but are not limited to so called macroeconomic issues (labor, regulations, impact of changing interest rates, consumer spending, fluctuations in currency), cyclicality, seasonality, suppliers or buyers, entry or exit costs, technology, competition, vulnerability to substitutes, and international considerations (if applicable). Many businesses operate on local or regional levels and events within certain company's market place affect it more than events in the country or abroad. Thus, focus on explaining to the lender the challenges and problems your business faces in its immediate market area.

3. Demonstrate what actions you have taken to mitigate main industry risks to help your company succeed

Please pay particular attention to the following: when you disclose an industry risk or anything that may be perceived as a risk (be objective and realistic), you MUST provide an explanation of how you have been able to mitigate and reduce or eliminate the risk. This is the key to giving lender confidence that you know what you are doing and are prepared to address and face the risks during the period of loan repayment. The list of mitigating factors can include your business' existing experience in dealing with some industry's challenges; the actions management is currently taking to address certain industry risks; or the game plan management developed to curb industry threats.

I would like to emphasize that you have to know your industry and know it well. It sounds simple but I have worked with enough borrowers who neglected to see and face their industry issues, which ultimately hurt their businesses. The next recommendation is to share during meetings with prospective lenders information about the industry dynamics and some of the key risks your company is facing. Do it before the lender learns about them on his or her own. Finally, explain and demonstrate on the basis of some of your business' achievements how you are prepared to face and mitigate those risks. If you follow these rather simple suggestions, you will make the lenders' job easier, will earn their respect, and will lay a foundation for your future loan relationship.

CHAPTER 24 – LENDERS' PERSONALITIES

In my banking career I have met lots of lenders with a wide range of personalities. However, I noticed some common traits that are summarized in personality profiles below. The reason why I have included this information in my book is simple: lenders manage your loan relationships, but you can also manage them to ensure that you receive the service and treatment you need and deserve. The lending profession has always been considered the cream-of-the-crop of the banking industry. Up until about the last ten years, candidates often spent a decade or more working for their companies prior to becoming lenders. This is typically one of the best-compensated jobs in the industry. By the same token, it is also the most stressful and demanding career in the industry. Lending officers juggle incredibly high sales goals while taking care of very demanding customers. They also deal with other factors: frequently they do not get enough administrative support to assist with their workloads, and they are constantly being watched by many federal and state regulators, internal review and compliance departments, and outside auditors. This will perhaps help explain why lenders behave the way they do.

Mr. or Mrs. Buddy
These lenders are very friendly, always pleasant, and available whenever you need them. You are always welcome. While it may seem that they are always on your side and will do anything for you, please be cautious. When it comes to meeting their performance goals and keeping their jobs, this is when the Buddy personality can disappear. Overall, I think they are easier to deal with, as they try to match your pace and tone whenever possible.

The cocky one
This type of lender is, in my experience, the one who knows his or her job very well. Otherwise, such a person would not last in his or her position. It is not always easy to deal with this personality type. These lending officers are very straightforward, bordering on arrogant,

and it is not always easy to understand their sense of humor. However, they know what they are doing and can get you the right services and products. If you are to continue having them as your lenders, you will either need to get used to their personalities or be frank with them that you do not appreciate such type of treatment. In the latter scenario, you may be surprised to find that because their personality can handle a frank request, you may end up with the best lender you can ask for.

The snooty know-it-all
In my opinion, this is perhaps the most difficult personality to deal with for both customers and colleagues. When they have an excellent day, they are the nicest people to deal with. However, most of the time they are reserved, lack emotion, are very proper, and are rather impersonal with their customers. When your business is doing well and the loans are not at risk, they treat you well. Once your company experiences financial difficulties or goes through challenging times, they will give you little slack and will make you feel that they are in control of the situation. I recommend not going out of your way to develop a personable relationship, but simply responding in the same way. I have also noticed that this personality type has little tolerance for customers who do not know their businesses or talk about a business topic they are not proficient in. Therefore, do not try to pretend that you are somebody you are not – use fewer words, more action.

The overwhelmed one
This is the lender who typically has too many customers, little administrative support, and simply can no longer handle the work volume and pressures that come with it. They may not be easy to reach or may not deliver a promised service on time. The good thing about this type of lender is that you will not be contacted by him or her for long periods of time, if you are one of those people who views calls from your lenders as a bother. The negative side is that you may get the impression that they do not care about your business. In their defense I would like to underline that they do care, although it may rarely be manifested in their actions.

The ultimate schmoozer

This is Mr. or Mrs. Charming. Unlike the Buddy personality, they do not try to become your best friend. On the contrary, their goal is to get your business and develop an excellent relationship without getting too close. It may feel like you are speaking with a close friend, but as soon as the conversation ends you may feel that you know nothing about them. You will have a very difficult time saying no, as you will feel that you are about to hurt the nicest person on earth. One thing you have to remember is to always hold your ground with this kind of lender. If you need time to think about something that is offered to you, be nice but firm.

The humble one

This type of lender is a minority because of the job demands discussed above. If you have a dominating, bossy personality, try to tone it down. While this lender will never tell you that they are not happy with how you treat them, their discontent may be reflected in the quality of service you receive. This lender is most proper and respectful of them all, but does not like to be taken advantage of.

When dealing with lenders you have two choices: you can either think that you are in charge and expect to get everything you want (it does not mean that you will always get it) or adjust your behavior to your lender's personality to ensure that you always get the type of service and attention you require. While the latter may sound difficult, I am confident that this is the best way to achieve the results you want from lenders. Chapter 32 will discuss how to behave if you are unhappy with your lender and your differences appear to be irreconcilable.

Chapter 25 – How Lenders Review Your Loan Request and What It Means to You

Each lending institution approaches the review of small business loan requests differently. However, there are a couple of clear trends that you should be aware of. You should have different strategies for how to approach those lenders based on how your prospective lender is likely to review, or what lenders call "underwrite", your loan requests.

To reduce costs and loan approval time, improve the quality of loans, and eliminate human subjectivity and judgment from decision making, lenders began to take advantage of technology in analyzing loan requests. The first steps were taken in the arena of consumer loans, but have now reached small business loans. Lending institutions developed various mathematical and statistical tools to help them quickly analyze business requests. The ultimate goal for lenders is to improve profitability. While some small businesses did benefit in the process, it is the lending institutions that became the main beneficiaries of this innovation.

"Scoring" is a term that is used more and more widely in the lending community. Scoring is essentially a method of entering certain pieces of financial and non-financial information about companies into a software program. The software assigns a score, which signals whether the loan should be made. While scoring can be traced back to the 1950s, it has been actively used in small business lending only in the last 10 to 15 years.[1] One of the main reasons why scoring has shifted from consumer to small business loans is because research uncovered a correlation between the two groups of borrowers.

Loan approval by large financial institutions, including banks

When I started my career in lending, most of the large banks were using scoring. At that point, many of those organizations were scoring term loan and line of credit requests with total loan amounts of up to

$100,000 to any small business. This means that if the total amount of loans with Bank A is not more than $100,000, including the new loan request, the loan request was scored. Now this threshold is being slowly pushed to $250,000 and even higher.

What this means to you is that your loan request is typically sent to a centralized underwriting hub, which could be hundreds of miles away from where you are. Employees there enter various information about your company into a software model that concludes whether your loan request should be approved or not. This information may consist of your company's financial ratios (liquidity or leverage as described in Chapter 7 under "scored underwriting"), the debt service coverage ratio (similar to the one described in Chapter 9), the number of years in business, sales and profitability trends, and the owner's personal credit score. These underwriting departments are focused processing as many loan requests as possible every day. They are not compensated according to how many loans are approved, but rather on making sure that their employer's interests are protected by extending loans to worthy business borrowers.

Benefits of scoring and centralized underwriting:
- Faster turnaround
- Streamlined and frequently simplified documentation requirements

Negatives of scoring and centralized underwriting:
- Lack of control from your lending officer or account manager
- No regard for qualitative factors and your business' specific situation
- Lower chances of approval if your business is experiencing financial difficulties

Loan approval by small community banks and other small lenders

Small banks and lending institutions tend to review small business loan requests in a less formalized way. They focus on analyzing your cash flow, financial performance, and the Cs of credit (see Chapter 17) just as they would analyze loan requests from large companies. Scoring software is too expensive for small lenders, whether they buy existing software products or develop their own. Your loan request will go to a lender, who personally or with the assistance of his or her staff will review or underwrite your request. If they are not yet comfortable with granting you a loan but are not ready to reject your request outright, they will commonly contact you for additional information.

Benefits of traditional, non-scored underwriting:
- More attention given to your business' particular situation and qualitative factors
- Your lender has the ability to control the underwriting process
- Your lender may be more flexible about your circumstances

Negatives of traditional, non-scored underwriting:
- Longer underwriting process
- Impact of human judgment on your loan request

Small lending institutions typically have an aura of being a part of the community. They market their services with a particular focus on the needs of small businesses and quick access to a human being during business hours. Large lenders are typically perceived as having a wide range of products and services, superior on-line capabilities, and 24-hour customer assistance by phone. As the competition is extremely strong, I am sure you will also hear the opposite claims. Keep in mind that with the scoring process you do not need to submit any written Request for Loan Proposal or business plan. They are not likely to be considered.

You should assess your loan approval chances based on the knowledge you acquire by reading this book. If your company's financial performance and cash flow are satisfactory, you should have a good chance for acquiring a loan with either large or small lenders. What you need to decide is whether your company's culture will have a better match with a larger or smaller lending institution. If your company's performance is less than satisfactory, but you believe that there are mitigating factors that are strong enough to mitigate the weaknesses, you may want to consider applying to lenders that do not utilize scored underwriting. Smaller lenders will most often be your choice for loan requests under $200,000 to $300,000, if your company is a start-up, has recently lost money, or otherwise does not fit the parameters of the scored loan approval. Just don't forget to ask your prospective lending officer whether loan requests of your size will be scored. Of course, if loan requests of your size are not scored, use the roadmap outlined in this book to improve your chances of getting your loan.

[1] "The Role of Credit Scores in Consumer Lending Today", article by Elizabeth Mays, October 2003, RMA Journal.

Other sources used:
"Microfinance: Part 2; Why and How", Gail Buyske, June 2004, RMA Journal.
"The Next Chapter in Small Business Scoring", Marcus Bishop, February 2002, RMA Journal.

FINDING A LENDER

CHAPTER 26 – ASSESSING YOUR CHANCES OF GETTING A LOAN

To objectively assess your chances of being approved for a loan you have to be honest in answering a series of questions. They deal with your company's cash flow, collateral, your financial strength as a guarantor, the equity in your business, management experience, and the risks involved in your industry.[1] This is a non-mathematical approach to evaluating your chances; however, it can be a powerful tool in assessing the strengths and weaknesses of your loan requests. In the table below, for each category insert one check mark to indicate "weak", "strong", or "satisfactory". Weakness in one category can be offset by strength in another. In addition, I recommend looking for possible mitigating factors directly in each weak category. For instance, your company has a weak, inadequate cash flow to cover proposed loan payments. Nonetheless, you recently acquired several new customers. As a result, your company's cash flow has improved substantially over the last several months and you can provide financial statements to prove it.

Category	Weak	Satisfactory	Strong	Mitigating factors, if weak
Cash flow				
Collateral				
Guarantor quality				
Equity in business				
Management				
Industry risks				
Total				

Cash flow – Perhaps the most powerful criterion. A weak cash flow means cash flow is not sufficient to cover your total expected debt payments. See Chapter 9-10 and Appendix 5 on how to calculate cash flow. Satisfactory cash flow will be at the debt service coverage ratio of 1.2:1 and up to about 2.0:1. Remember that one of the ways to calculate debt service coverage is by dividing your annual operating cash flow after financing by the expected annual loan payments, as discussed previously. Ratios of 2.0:1 and higher will be particularly strong and less than 1.2:1 will be weak.[2]

Collateral - Perhaps the second most important criterion, as it is expected to repay your loan if your company is unable to generate enough cash to make payments. As discussed in Chapter 12, only certain assets will likely be considered by lenders as something they could use as collateral to repay your loan. You should also recall that lenders discount those assets, because in a sell-off situation they are not likely to get the full market value. After you reduce or discount your assets, divide that amount by your total expected loans. If the ratio is 1:1 or less, your collateral is weak. If you do not really have any assets that can be viewed as collateral, again this category is weak. If your ratio is somewhere between 1.2:1 and 2.0:1, your collateral is satisfactory. A ratio above 2.0:1 should be strong.[2]

Guarantor quality – This category is harder to measure than the previous one, as lenders differ on how to they evaluate your guarantees. In addition, the strength of your guarantee will fluctuate based on the total loan amount. For example, if you personally own $100,000 in cash and marketable securities, applying for a $70,000 loan will likely make you look good as a guarantor. It would not look as favorable if you are applying for a $500,000 loan. Lenders traditionally look at your so-called liquid assets, personal net worth, and personal credit score to assess your ability to guarantee business loans. When your personal guarantee is a relying factor, lenders also evaluate your personal cash flow. The goal is to calculate how much so-called excess cash your household has after paying taxes, personal debt payments, and all living expenses.

Your personal liquidity is traditionally evaluated by evaluating your liquid assets (cash, marketable securities, and the like) and by calculating your liquidity or crash ratio. The ratio is calculated by dividing your liquid assets by your personal current liabilities or debt payments due in the next 12 months. The goal is to determine whether you will be able to meet your personal debt payments in the next 12 months from your savings, if you regular income flow is interrupted. Ratio of less than one is weak; between 1.0:1 and 1.2:1 is adequate; between 1.2:1 and 2.0:1 is satisfactory or good; and greater than 2.0 is strong. The ratio ranges were provided as a guideline only and may not be followed by all lenders. However, the goal is to have the crash ratio of greater than one.

Lenders also evaluate your personal net worth. Similar to the business net worth calculations, the personal net worth is estimated by the following formula: personal assets *minus* personal liabilities *equals* personal net worth. As explained in Chapter 13, some assets, such as personal belongings and autos, are excluded from this analysis. After determining your personal net worth, lenders may calculate your equity ratio: net worth *divided* by total assets. The rule of thumb is to have 50% or more in equity. Liquidity and personal net worth evaluations are rather gray areas, and there are no clear guidelines within the lending community on what is strong, weak, or average. As for your personal credit score, the score of less than 650 is typically viewed as weak. If your score is between 650 and 750, you are regarded as an average quality guarantor. Above 750 is strong. See Chapter 13 and 14 for more information.

Equity in business – This category looks at what would be left of your business assets, if all liabilities were to be repaid. This is your equity, a.k.a. business net worth. Note that lenders exclude from your assets goodwill or other intangible assets in order to calculate what we know as tangible net worth. Negative net worth is a clear weakness. Negative net worth is quite common for real estate investment companies, but lenders do not like to see negative net worth in most other industries. Net worth of about 20% to 30% is considered to be satisfactory. Less than 20% to 30% is on the weaker side. Greater than 30% is viewed to be strong. Lenders also often refer to the RMA Annual Statement Studies, which contain comparative data for businesses in various industries. The goal is to compare your company to other companies in your area of expertise. At times, net worth data in individual industries will vary from the suggested net worth percentages above. In addition, cash basis financial statements may not show some of your assets, such as accounts receivable. However, the above guideline is a good starting point.

Management qualities – This area is frequently overlooked and underestimated by small business owners. Being proficient or even excelling in a trade does not guarantee business success. Neither do management skills alone without knowledge of the trade. You should ensure that you have people on your team who have management experience. It is hardest to do if you are a small business, particularly a one-man or one-woman show. Lenders assess management skills by looking at your company's financial achievements, management positions held at other companies, and the references of partners, business associates, or employers. Lenders will ask themselves whether you will be successful in organizing your operations, managing time and stress, motivating and inspiring employees, delivering your products and services to your customers and keeping them happy.

Industry risks – This is also a very qualitative category. It is not possible to attach a number to it, unless you decide to compare your income statement and balance sheet ratios to those of your industry. Each industry has many risks, but you should easily be able to identify the two or three most significant. If you have nothing in place to reduce or mitigate those risks, your company is viewed as a weak loan candidate. If the measures you have in place can reduce or eliminate the main risks, your risk profile is satisfactory. If you are able to significantly reduce the key risks and they are no longer a threat, your risk profile is strong.

The last step in this section is to tally all the weak, satisfactory, and strong categories. If you have four or more weak categories, there may be clear signs that you are not likely to qualify for a business loan. This is particularly true if your weaknesses are in the first three categories. Your next steps will be to rethink your loan request and to spend time on improving your company's cash flow. In addition, you may need to put more equity into your company. Other options include finding more collateral, particularly cash or marketable securities. You should only offer cash and other liquid assets as collateral if you are confident that your business will generate positive cash flow rather soon. This means that you have good chances of getting your collateral back after the loans are repaid. You may also improve your chances by having a very financially strong guarantor support your loan request.

With two to three weak categories, you may get your loan request approved, but I recommend looking for those additional mitigating factors, particularly improving your cash flow.

With mostly satisfactory and strong categories, if you assessed them conservatively and realistically, you should not have a hard time getting your loan request approved. Of course, your request should demonstrate satisfactory business cash flow to cover payments. When things look good, there is no reason to relax. It takes considerable effort to maintain steady financial performance or improve your company's finances.

---

[1] This is a list of key areas of analysis for many lenders. Note, however, that some lenders may choose to analyze other or additional criteria.
[2] This is my definition of satisfactory, strong, and weak cash flow and collateral coverage. Some of my colleagues may disagree.

CHAPTER 27 – CHOICE OF LENDERS AND CREDIT PRODUCTS

This chapter is an overview of what is available to you, the small business owner, in the lending world. There are usually up to a dozen small business lenders chasing the same companies at any given point of time. Many more lenders target small businesses through the internet, mail campaigns, and various forms of advertising. These lenders range from local community and national banks with offices in your area, to global financing and credit card companies, to small business and community development corporations with locations locally or even hundreds of miles away, to private lenders. The range of products and services is also constantly expanding, although the basis for many loan products are the same traditional lines of credit, term loans, and mortgages that existed for quite some time.

Lenders

Your first choice is various large national (sometimes even international) and local community banks. Finding their names is not a chore, as you see their signs in your local area. For example, in the area of Boston, MA, we have several national and regional banks such as Bank of America, Citizens Bank, Sovereign Bank, and Bank North. While there are other full-service financial institutions, these are the names I see most of the time. In addition to these large companies, there are also small community banks. If we take Cambridge, MA for the sake of example (part of the greater Boston area), you are likely to see names such as Cambridge Savings, Cambridge Trust, Century, East Cambridge Savings, Wainwright, and several other smaller banks.

Besides seeing or hearing the names of lenders in your area, there are other ways of creating a list of your potential lenders. A telephone directory is a good source. Unfortunately, some tend to list businesses that pay listing fees, some of which may not specialize in business loans or may not be lenders at all. However, most banks and some credit unions do offer loans to small businesses. The internet is another source. You can look up names of banks in the same way you look up names in the telephone directory. Search engines such as Yahoo Yellow Pages, Google Local, Excite Yellow Pages, and others provide contact information to reach lenders in your area. Again, the drawback is that they list names of financial services institutions that may not even be in the business of offering small business loans. Therefore, when using those sources, your safest bet is to focus on banks and possibly credit unions.

In the instances when you are not satisfied with the choice of banks in your area or are unable to procure loans through the ones you applied to, the internet is a powerful tool. It can help you reach your goal of securing a loan or may become a source of aggravation. When you go to a search engine and type in a phrase such as "small business loans", you receive results from true small business lenders and various other financial and even non-financial service providers.

When you are looking up lenders by a general phrase that does not specify your location, your search will yield various organizations that may include loan brokers (middlemen), financial companies (non-banks), credit education and credit repair websites, financiers who bundle financing and non-financing services, factoring companies (non-financing, rather receivables buyers), small business grant-writing organizations, loan package software creators, and the list goes on and on. You will probably say – enough already! I could not agree more. For all the benefits the internet provides, it can get ugly out there. You want a simple loan, but get all these other products and services that you do not need. However, even when you specify your location in the search engine, you still get a good-sized list that goes beyond just lending companies and includes financial and non-financial organizations that can make your search very aggravating.

Loan types

To help you eliminate information overload and the potential confusion discussed in the previous paragraphs, you should learn to sift through information and pick only what is useful and applicable to your particular case. The first question to ask yourself is whether the company you are looking at is in the business of providing loans. This information can typically be found when you read about the company's products and services in the description of the company's business, or in speaking with its representatives. When searching for loans, also make sure that you are being offered loans, not grants, equity, or other non-loan products. For example, factoring your business accounts receivables is often mistaken for or misrepresented as a loan. Well, it is nothing but the sale of your receivables at a discount. In addition, small business grants are usually not loans. If the company on your radar screen is not in a lending business, move on.

The second question is to find out whether those loan or credit products and services are what you are looking for. You should start by looking at loan types and loan features. Here is a list of the most common types of loans: lines of credit, letters of credit, time notes, term loans, mortgages, leases, and credit cards. They are described in Chapter 7. All the other fancy names that lenders use for their loans are usually not loan types but loans with some additional features. For instance, an SBA loan is not a loan type but rather a guarantee attached to the loan that offers lenders stronger collateral. SBA 7A and 504 loan programs are also not loan types. The loans are still the same term loans and lines of credit with purposes and features that distinguish them from non-SBA-guaranteed loans.

Another example is asset-based loans, which most frequently consist of lines of credit and, less frequently, of term loans. The loan type is still lines of credit or term loans with money being advanced against your collateral (accounts receivable, inventory, etc), and those collateral balances are closely watched by your lenders. Some other loans with special features include supplier financing, equipment financing (leases and purchase financing), and inventory financing; however, these are still the same traditional lines of credit, term loans, and letters of credit. Furthermore, specific industry loans such as retailer, airline, and franchise financing are nothing more than the conventional loans discussed above with features that make them attractive to businesses in particular industries.

When you are searching for the right loan product, I recommend asking yourself if a loan is all you are looking for. Is the lowest pricing your only motivator, or will you need other loan, deposit, and cash management services? If you are looking for more than pricing, you should look at the other services lenders are offering. You may not take advantage of them immediately but may need them in the near future.

It is not easy to move an already existing relationship from one lender to another. Thus, think one step ahead. The ability to understand loan or credit products behind fancy names is a valuable skill. What is the type and purpose of the loan and what kinds of companies does it target? Make sure it is debt financing, if this is what you are looking for. Some loan brokers or loan intermediaries may take your company's information to solicit both. Also be careful about entering your data on websites that solicit lenders' interest. You may come across loan brokers or even financing organizations that are transaction oriented and may not spend time to understand your needs. The key is not to get intimidated by the names of loan products and services, to be able to understand their essence and purpose, not to dwell too long on services you do not understand, and move through your search at a relatively fast pace.

Chapter 28 – Loans from Relatives, Friends, and Other Private Individuals

Small business loans from family and friends, or so-called F&F loans, deserve a separate discussion. Some experts advise that these loans should be your last resort, while others advocate that this should be your first choice, and a relatively easy source of financing. In reality, you should decide what works best for your company, as there is no right or wrong choice as long as you understand the benefits and dangers of obtaining F&F loans. Private loans from people other than family and friends are frequently included in the F&F category.

My goal is to show you the pros and cons of F&F loans, so you can make an educated decision whether these loans are in the best interest of your business. Note that if you properly devise and document your private loan arrangement, the positives and negatives of debt financing discussed in Chapter 1 will also apply.

Family loans: pros and cons

Cons:
- Your family and friends frequently have a hard time saying no and an even harder time saying yes
- The possibility of permanently severing a valuable personal relationship
- In exchange for loans, family and friends tend to meddle in your business affairs, interfere with your management, and even question your personal spending
- The choice of prospective lenders is limited to the people you know well
- Lenders may feel that they are entitled to share your company's financial successes
- F&F loans traditionally do not allow your business to build a credit history

Pros:
- Quick, flexible, and frequently the cheapest source of loans
- No research is necessary to identify a quick list of prospective lenders
- No formal process for loan approval
- Frequently rewarding to your family and friends, giving them a sense of contribution to your success, if the loans are repaid as agreed
- Often the only source of financing for start-up businesses

In my experience, many small business entrepreneurs turned to F&F loans after they exhausted their options with traditional lenders. In those instances I frequently hear comments similar to: "To banks and government institutions like the SBA, they (entrepreneurs) are not gray and fat enough to be taken seriously." [1] As many entrepreneurs have discovered from their own experience, securing F&F or other private loans is not an easy task and requires knowledge and strategy. Your goal is twofold: 1) to make the person you are asking for a loan comfortable with your request and 2) to document your loan properly to protect yourself and your company from potential personal and legal battles.

Make the person you are asking for a loan comfortable with your request

As a first step, you should create a list of likely lenders. Determine their level of financial sophistication and what may motivate them to give you a loan. Start with family members and friends and finish with business associates, acquaintances, and other private individuals. Be cautious about borrowing from people you are very close to and people you know nothing about. You risk ruining a special relationship or asking for money from people who may not be trustworthy. The people in the middle tend to be a safer bet. Your character is what family and friends will be looking at first and foremost when lending you money.

When reviewing the list of your candidate lenders, be ethical and considerate. Do not ask for loans from people who either cannot afford to give you money or cannot afford to lose a loan, if your company fails. For instance, your elderly grandparents with limited retirement savings are probably not a good source of loans. If they rely on their savings for living expenses, tying that money up in a loan may not be in their best financial interest. Never pressure people into lending you money. If lenders feel that the decision to lend was not their own, you may soon find yourself in the center of personal and even legal battles. Finally, allow your prospects to reject your loan request and be able to accept the rejection, without damaging your relationship.

The second step is to present your loan request. Your presentation should consist of two parts: verbal pitch and written follow-up. Verbal or face-to-face presentation sets the goal of giving a brief overview of your request and gauging the level of interest. Some industry experts describe this meeting as an opportunity for a prospective lender to look into your eyes. Talk about your business background, your management experience and how it will help assure the success of your company, your business goals for the next two-three years, and the financing you seek. Is your prospective lender interested? If yes, explain that you would like to sign a loan agreement, which will outline the loan amount, loan purpose, interest rate, repayment plan, and other details that will help ensure timely loan repayment. Also be clear that you are requesting a loan, which does not constitute ownership in your company or management responsibilities. Explain some of the risks and how you are prepared to reduce or eliminate them.

A written presentation should follow your in-person presentation. The goal of the follow-up is to allow your prospective lenders to make their decision. Your verbal pitch will excite interest and a written follow-up document is to cement that interest and a desire to give you the money.

Should you prepare a formal Request for Loan Proposal? I certainly think you should. However, it does not have to be as extensive as the one you will prepare for traditional lenders. The focus is on outlining your loan request, your credentials and expertise, and your business goals. A reader of your RLP should have a clear understanding of what will make your business successful and allow you to repay the loan as promised. Of course, providing some financial information is helpful, but your family and friends are probably less financially savvy than traditional lenders and would not need to conduct the same financial analysis. Nevertheless, feel free to include the financial analysis, if you believe that it will add strength to your loan request.

Document your loan properly

Documenting your loan arrangement is one of the most crucial aspects of securing loans; it will protect you and your lenders from misunderstandings and disputes. Even if your prospective lender swears that there is no need to have a formal agreement, do it to protect your personal possessions and your business. Be as explicit as possible. The loan agreement should state the loan amount, loan purpose, term of the loan, methods and dates of repayment, interest rate, collateral and guarantees, if any, the rights and responsibilities of the borrower and lender, and provisions in case of default. Also consider having a clause that requires one or both parties to forfeit rights to a court proceeding and to resolve disputes through a mediator. Some borrowers have gone so far as to require that a lender never mention in public the fact that he or she gave them a loan.[2] You will be better served by hiring a qualified attorney to prepare and sign the loan documents, as legal issues tend to be complex. They frequently vary from state to state and legal advice could prove to be invaluable.

The tax impact of private loans should also be taken into consideration. Some lenders may be tempted to grant a loan and charge a minimal interest rate, or none at all. Granting a loan with an interest rate less than the IRS's Applicable Federal Rates (AFR) or no interest at all may be subject to imputed income and gift taxes for your lender. Experts indicate that to avoid imputed income and gift taxes and other consequences and to ensure the tax deductibility of interest in your business' financial statements, you should do the following: propose an interest rate equal to or greater than AFR, show the loan amount, have defined payment dates, specify if security or guarantee exist, and otherwise show that you have a true lender-borrower relationship (see IRS Publication 550).[3] Instruct your lender to write a memo stating that you, the borrower, were solvent at the time the loan was made. Of course, do this only if it is true. These actions allow the lender to avoid the IRS's imputed taxes by establishing that the borrower intends to repay the debt and the lender intends to collect it. As this matter can be complex, I suggest seeking the advice of a qualified tax adviser.

Final thoughts and suggestions

An alternative way to borrow money from your family and friends is by asking them to pledge their marketable securities, such as stocks or bonds. A traditional lender, such as a community bank, will take those securities as collateral and give you a loan. You can also negotiate that some of those stocks or bonds are released back to their owners as you reduce the loan balance.[4] The trick is to repay the loan or your family and relatives will lose their investments. While the loan does not come from your family or friends, they make it possible. You should sign an agreement outlining the nature of your arrangement and the rights and responsibilities of both parties involved.

Shy away from interest-only F&F loans and do your best to repay the principal. I agree with finance experts who recommend using family and friends' money only for short periods of time and on a very limited basis. Switch to a conventional lender as soon as the opportunity arises, unless you are absolutely happy with the private loan arrangement.[5]

When presenting your loan requests to candidates, offer more than one loan option: a higher interest rate on longer term loans and a lower interest rate on shorter term loans. Consider mortgage style payments; equal payment amounts with more going toward interest in the beginning and more toward principal at the end. You may consider an interest-only option for a period of time, before repayment of principal begins. **Always test your repayment ability against the cash flow you expect to produce.** For instance, a loan of $50,000 to expand a daycare facility could have several repayment options: 1) Interest only in the first year with $12,500 in principal in each of the remaining four years plus interest; 2) Principal payments of $8,333 in each of 6 years plus interest; 3) Principal payment of $10,000 in each of the first two years plus interest and principal payments of $15,000 in the remaining two years plus interest. You create the options and your prospective lender makes the choice.

If your lender needs a sweetener to seal the deal, offer attractive interest rates in the range of what traditional lenders charge or even higher. If F&F lenders are your only choice, perhaps you should offer a higher return. This is of course if you and your company can afford making those payments. Also consider offering your lenders a closing fee, from several hundred to a thousand dollars or higher, if again a fee might cement their desire to give you money. Offer to include in loan documentation covenants that will make the loan more attractive. Covenants may call for minimum quarterly or annual business profits or regular submission of your company's financial statements (annual, quarterly, or some other frequency). Do not volunteer too much, if it is not in your company's best interest. However, keep these options in your mind as possible points to negotiate.

Family, friends, and other private lenders may question your determination to make timely loan payments. In addition, lenders want to avoid the unpleasant experience of collecting delinquent loans. Loan administration companies help small business owners overcome lenders' hesitation. A good example is Circle Lending of Waltham, MA, which helps small business owners prepare loan documentation and collect payments, provides statements, offers on-line access to the loan information for both borrowers and lenders, and files collateral liens on behalf of your lenders with state agencies. It even reports your payment behavior to credit agencies, helping you and your company build a credit history. Circle Lending's services give private lenders added assurance that their loans will be repaid.

---

[1] "What Would You do for Start-Up Cash? From Pilfering Paper Clips to Mingling with Movie Stars, Here are 8 Entrepreneurs' Never-Say-Die Financing Strategies"; by Christopher Lancette; Business Start-Ups magazine, January 1999.

[2] "I Have to Borrow Capital from a Relative. Any Tips?", by Jill Andresky Fraser; Inc magazine, February 1997.

[3] "Fool.com: Family Loans", by Roy Lewis; www.fool.com, August 1999.

[4] "Borrowing: A Different Twist on Family Loans", by Jill Andresky Fraser; Inc magazine, June 1996.

[5] "Raising Capital: How to Borrow from Family and Friends", by Jill Andresky Fraser; Inc magazine, July 1995.

Chapter 29 – Pre-interviews of Lenders

Even if your loan request is only for $10,000, you should consider pre-interviewing prospective lenders to learn a bit about their organizations and account officers, services and products, and expectations. This process may only require 5 to 10 minutes to make arrangements to speak with a representative and a 10 to 15 minute conversation. Some of the main benefits of learning about your prospective lenders prior to applying are: the chance to learn about their loans, how long it will take to review a loan request, what information is required from you, what types of products and services they offer in addition to loans, what their expectations are for new borrowers, how their customer service is structured and the hours it is available, and even something as simple as the level of energy you sense from speaking with a representative or a lender of that company.

Whether your company is a good or weak candidate for a loan, most often lenders will not give you a commitment to lend during a preliminary conversation. Considering the level of competition among lenders for new business loans, they will be delighted to speak with any potential customer. However, you should get just enough information about the candidate to help you make your final decision: Do I want to apply with this lender? Here are some questions I recommend asking during your conversation:

- How much experience do you and your company have in lending to businesses in my industry of similar revenue size? (This helps you to anticipate whether the lender can understand and address your company's loan and non-loan needs.)
- Do you extend loans of this amount? (Some lenders may not lend outside of a certain loan size.)
- Do you finance this kind of loan purpose? (You will have to know what that purpose is.)
- If my company borrows from your organization, will my employees and I have access to a dedicated loan officer for our

customer service needs? May I speak with him or her?
- What loan and non-loan products and services do you offer?
- What financial statements do you require to apply for a loan with your company?
- What are your organization's strengths? What are its weaknesses?
- Will you be able to ensure a smooth, uninterrupted transfer of my existing loans, deposits, and other services? How will you achieve that?

You may further expand or tailor this list to your particular needs. I recommend limiting the number of questions you ask to five to seven, out of respect for the lenders' time and your own. Focus on issues that are most important to you. While you may feel somewhat awkward during the first couple of conversations due to lack of experience, I am confident that you will soon be able to figure out what questions matter the most. If you choose to conduct preliminary interviews or apply immediately after you identify the names of potential lending institutions, the table below will help you structure and organize your search. I strongly encourage you to modify the table to your company's needs and your personal preferences. The next chapter will help organize the search for lenders and will add discipline to your efforts to secure loans.

Loan Financing Guide for Small Business Owners

Lending company name	Contact name / phone # or email	Location	Information required to apply	Impression of the lending officer (Scale 1-10)	Comments: date of conversation, responses, conversation summary, etc.

CHAPTER 30 – CHOOSING AND APPLYING

When searching for prospective lenders and applying for loans, you must be organized and keep track of your workflow. Securing loan financing can be a very time-consuming process, and meticulous record-keeping of everything you do is the only effective solution I can recommend. You will save time and money and eliminate many stressful and frustrating moments. The table presented in this chapter is one possible way of staying in control.

Step 1 – Choose three to five lending organizations from the names you have already identified. This is a manageable number that gives you choices and keeps you from turning your search into a full-time endeavor.

Step 2 – Gather the financial statements that are required to apply. These financial statements typically include two to three of the most recent years of your company's tax returns, two to three of the most recent years of the principal's tax returns (if the principal is planning on guaranteeing the loan), and possibly interim, management-prepared financial statements. Lending institutions will also have their own applications and forms, such as a loan application, personal financial statement, and others.

Step 3 – Create a timeline to apply and receive responses about your loan requests. You should expect that from the moment you apply and submit all necessary financial statement it typically takes two to seven business days to get an answer; in some rare instances up to two weeks.

The table at the end of this chapter will help you gather the information you are likely to need at this stage. You may recreate it in Excel, a word processing program, or write it on paper, if you still prefer to do things without a computer. I do encourage you to modify this table to your needs and focus on the sections that are most valuable to your particular situation. Once you have obtained the information you need and have submitted all the statements required to apply, set follow-up dates to ensure that you do not lose track of the application process. As your prospective lenders are working on reviewing your loan requests, your job is to compare the information you have gathered, to rate lenders in the order they appeal to you. You may not receive a loan from the lending institution you really liked. However, you will still know who, in your opinion, looks more appealing if you are given a choice. Once you have submitted your loan package and you are waiting for the responses, your job is done, and it is up to lenders to do theirs. If you feel that it is taking longer than expected, you should take the matter into your own hands and follow up.

Remember that many lenders charge fees to apply. They may also require a commitment fee to compensate for their time and to ensure that you are serious and not just shopping around. Look for and choose your lenders wisely.

Loan Financing Guide for Small Business Owners

Lending company name	Contact name / phone # or email	Location	Information required to apply	Impression of the lending officer (Scale 1-10)	Comments: date of conversation, responses, conversation summary, etc.

Continuation

Next follow up date	Possible loan pricing	Loan fees	Deposit services	Minimum balances / fees	Other services	Comments

MORE USEFUL INFORMATION

CHAPTER 31 – BEING HONEST WITH LENDERS IN GOOD TIMES AND IN BAD TIMES; PROS AND CONS

In lenders' opinion, the pillars of satisfactory loan repayment are honest communication on the part of small business owners. Honesty and ethical behavior are such worn out topics that you may think they have nothing to do with how you handle your loans and communicate with your loan officers. On the contrary, they are the crux of lenders' willingness to finance your business needs.

When your company is performing well financially, when it generates sufficient profits and cash flow, and when loan repayment is not threatened, you can certainly get away with some things without jeopardizing your loan relationship. However, a loan officer will make note of your behavior for the future. If your company's financial performance deteriorates or a loan repayment is threatened, that nice individual you call "my-favorite-lender-who-forgives-me-everything" can turn into your biggest nightmare. If your lender believes that you have been dishonest in the past, he or she would think that you are likely to be dishonest during difficult times.

Here are several examples of what can be viewed as dishonest and unethical behavior:

- Purposefully delaying submission of financial statements to conceal that your company has been losing money.
- Borrowing money for one reason but spending it on something else, particularly unrelated to your business.
- Changing ownership in your company without permission of your lender, when your loan agreement stipulates that you have to secure such permission.
- Borrowing more money from new lenders without notifying your existing ones, when your loan agreement prohibits such actions.
- Cleaning your company's cash to satisfy your personal spending habits and then borrowing money to fill in cash flow gaps.

- Not disclosing potentially damaging situations that lenders can eventually discover on their own. This includes the loss of a significant customer or supplier, which can adversely impact your company's revenue and profitability; an impending law suit that can have a negative effect on your company's financial health; potentially damaging developments in your industry; and personal situations that are likely to hurt your business' financial health.

If you notice, these examples are milder in potential impact than committing a fraud or other financial crimes (although some may be viewed as illegal). Many of these situations can and will eventually be discovered in your financial statements and credit reports. The above examples are red flags for lenders, and concealing problems is a poor long-term solution to your business problems.

When your company is in trouble, enlisting lenders' cooperation is highly important, as they may be a vital player in your company's survival. Each time your company borrows money, it faces risks and derives benefits, and you should have a clear understanding of both. Here are the key risks and benefits of being honest with your creditors.

Risks of being honest with lenders:

- Lenders may limit their desire to give you money in the future, if they know that their existing loan repayment is already in jeopardy.
- Lenders may begin to look for additional collateral, if they feel that the existing collateral is not adequate.
- Lenders may request additional financial information, meet to discuss an already unpleasant topic, bring more attention to your loan relationship that may put some psychological pressure on you, ask you to communicate strategies to resolve the problems, and closely monitor the progress of your efforts.
- If your company is already in financial trouble but is not yet defaulting on its loans, some lenders may take it a step further and ask you to take your business elsewhere.

Benefits of being honest with lenders:

- Secure the lenders' willingness to be patient and work with your company when it is going through difficult times.
- Gives lenders a chance to offer alternatives that are often mutually beneficial and allow you to preserve your loan relationship (e.g. restructure your loan term and payment amount).
- Provides lenders with additional confidence that your character and integrity will help ensure successful loan repayment.
- Frequently gives you the necessary time to improve the situation and avoid some of the worst outcomes related to borrowing money, such as bankruptcy and sale of your business assets.[1]

While the risks presented above may seem to be a strong deterrent from keeping your lenders informed about your business and even certain personal situations, loan officers believe that the benefits outweigh the risks. To test this commonly known theory, I reached out to about a dozen of senior, experienced lenders located in Massachusetts, New York, California, Texas, Florida, and Ohio. Without any surprise, lenders responded in a remarkable unison despite their different locations and backgrounds. The main conclusion – it is very important to keep lenders appraised of your company's financial health, particularly when it is experiencing or is likely to face financial problems.

Each lender recommended looking for solutions to your company's challenges as early as possible and with your lender's direct involvement. The respondents were in agreement that concealing truth will only lead to your lender's adverse reaction and dissuade them from working with you. However, an advance notice of impending problems will give both the lender and the small business owner a chance to save the loan relationship and your business.

In conclusion, here are the words of advice from one of the lenders that is representative of the opinions of other lending officers: "Timing is everything in meeting the challenges of running a business, and this includes admitting you have a problem when one exists. If you are not sure, talk to your lender or another member of the "team". Don't treat

D. Neil Berdiev

your lenders as if they are your favorite mushrooms (kept in the dark and fed some manure)."[2]

[1] In certain situations, particularly such as possible bankruptcy or grave financial problems, I also recommend contacting a lawyer and a financial adviser to develop a strategy that suits your company.
[2] The survey is confidential and does not disclose the names of lenders or their companies as a condition of participation.

CHAPTER 32 – MANAGING YOUR SATISFACTION WITH LENDERS

You periodically review your relationship with suppliers, customers, and even business associates: you make changes that better serve your company or choose to establish new relationships. Similarly, you should monitor your level of satisfaction with your lenders. As I described previously, competition among lenders has become highly intense. Many of them are willing to undercut interest rates and fees to win your company's business. In addition, lenders are quick to match each other's products and services, frequently turning them into a commodity. Take advantage of this environment, if you are unhappy with your existing relationship.

I included several questions below that can help you periodically evaluate your existing relationship and decide whether you want to continue with your existing lender or find a new one. Problems arise in any business relationship. What is important is your lender's ability to address and resolve those problems to your satisfaction in a timely matter. My recommendation is to always communicate with your lenders about the issues that you are not satisfied with. I suggest letting them know, proactively, what you are looking for – after all, it is in your lender's interest to find solutions. If the response or outcome is unacceptable to you, with the help of the questions below you should determine if you are prepared to take the next step – moving your relationship to a new lender.

- Is your loan or account officer knowledgeable and professional, yet friendly? How is this important to you?
- Does your lender truly understand your loan and other service needs? How does he or she meet them?
- How competitive do you believe the pricing and selection of the products and services are as compared to your lender's competitors?
- Is your loan officer or another associate of the organization available when you need him or her?

- Is your lender able to resolve your problems in a timely manner?

Moving your relationship is not easy, for a number of reasons. When lenders win your loan business, they also try to cross-sell various other services, including cash management, deposit, credit cards, and payroll. They do it because this is often the only way to create a profitable relationship. Moreover, it is difficult for you to move the entire ballooned relationship elsewhere, when you are not satisfied with its quality. The difficulty of moving your relationship, including service interruption, is perhaps the key reason why lenders are so aggressive in promoting a variety of products. Thus, the decision to move should be a well thought-out one.

Prior to putting your loan business on the market, consider communicating your dissatisfaction to your lending officer. In addition to demonstrating your dissatisfaction, you should highlight the benefits of keeping your company's business. For example, you should mention anything from interest expenses, fees, or deposit balances you maintained over a period of time. In addition, if you consistently repaid loans as agreed, were a long-time, loyal customer, or referred business prospects that resulted in new loans to your lending institution, bring that information to the table to support your argument. Once you have expressed your concerns, evaluate whether your loan officer is able and willing to resolve your problems. I recommend not only expressing displeasure, but also suggesting possible ways to solve problems. If you believe that the attempts to salvage your loan relationship did not produce the desired results, you should take active steps to identify a new lender and move your entire relationship as fast as possible. Once you have identified potential lenders, it is crucial to inquire how prospective lenders can ensure a smooth transfer. See Chapters 29 and 30 for more information.

Chapter 33 – Negotiating Pricing

Lenders, just like small business owners, focus more and more on becoming and remaining profitable. Who can blame them? Competition is more intense than ever. Customers, including small businesses, are more sophisticated and demanding. They keep switching from lender to lender in search of the lowest pricing. Developments in technology and the underwriting process allow lenders to approve better-quality loan prospects faster than in the past.

Lending institutions vary in the way they make money on loans. Loan revenue typically comes from interest and fees. Interest has traditionally been the main source of income. However, the low interest environment and competition have changed it all. Fees are becoming an increasingly valuable source of income for lenders. In addition, a growing number of lending institutions not only set new loan goals for their lending officers, but also require them to meet fee goals. When you think that you have received the lowest interest rate, take a look at fee schedules for loan and even non-loan products.

While it is unreasonable to expect that lenders will cut their interest and fees to a minimum, you can and should negotiate loan pricing. The greater the amount of your loan, the more valuable those savings are. Lending institutions and their lending officers vary in their ability to reduce pricing. However, there is often some leeway. I assume that you have evaluated your company's financial condition and your chances of getting a loan, as described earlier in the book. The stronger your qualities as a prospective borrower, the greater leverage you have (see Chapter 26 on how to evaluate your qualities). Similar to the approach discussed in the previous chapter, show your prospective lending officer what you will bring to the table. The list might begin with the quality of your company's financial condition and collateral and continue to loan amounts, deposit accounts, and other services that are likely to generate income for the lending institution.

Loan pricing can be floating or fixed. For lines of credit and term loans, you will most frequently encounter floating pricing. Lenders pick some base or starting rate, such as prime rate or the LIBOR rate and then usually add a spread that could be 1% to 3% or even higher. The total rate (base rate plus or minus the spread) compensates lenders for the risks they take lending you money. The riskier your business and the loan structure are, the higher the total rate is likely to be. As I mentioned previously, loan pricing may include various fees. Some examples of fees are the application fee, underwriting fee, commitment fee, and renewal fee. Therefore, when negotiating to lower your interest rate, do not forget about fees. When lenders are not able or willing to reduce the interest rate they charge you, they may be able to reduce or waive fees. The total cost of your loan is the total of interest and fees.

Remember that when you are negotiating loan pricing, there is no harm done in pressing hard. Nevertheless, all depends on how professional you are, as disrespectful behavior can lead to the erosion of any rapport you might have established with the loan officer. Do not forget that getting him or her on your side is the best thing you can do, during and after the loan search process. In certain situations when you feel that a lending officer is not able to bend any further, it is your turn to either take the deal or choose other options.

In conclusion, I would like to mention that some lenders pursue active pricing management. You are not likely to encounter it with loans around $100,000 or less. Active pricing management entails a changing spread that is added to the base rate based on your company's financial performance. For instance, if you have a profitable year and have paid in a timely manner, the lender may lower your rate from prime plus 2% to prime plus 1%. This is a way to reward good financial performance. The opposite is true in a bad year. Based on my experiences, a small but growing group of lenders use this approach. However, I foresee that this may change in the near future, as lenders continue to reward some types of behavior, while discouraging others. If your lender utilizes active pricing management, nothing precludes you from trying to negotiate your interest and fees even in a bad year, although you may have less success in such circumstances. Threatening to leave is not likely to help. Your lender knows that businesses that experience financial difficulties are not welcome guests at other lending institutions.

CHAPTER 34 – OTHER VALUABLE POINTS

We have covered a vast amount of ground, from evaluating whether loan financing is right for your company to how to prepare a powerful Request for Loan Proposal. While it is not possible to discuss every single scenario related to obtaining and repaying loans, hopefully, this book has given you all the fundamental knowledge you need to bring you success. In this chapter, I would like to offer you some valuable pointers that came from lessons learned by small business owners and their lenders.

Loans are available when you do NOT need them
Some small business customers of my banks had lines of credit that they used very rarely. A number of those companies had never borrowed money before, while they could have easily qualified for term loans, mortgages, and other loans up to a certain dollar amount. These were profitable companies and had no need to borrow money. However, the financial fortunes of small companies can change from time to time and businesses can find themselves in situations when their financial health deteriorates. To the great surprise of those companies' owners and managers, lenders will then be reluctant to grant them loans.

This is the "beauty" of borrowing money. When you don't need it, it is available. When you must have it, it is hard to come by. Why? The answer is simple. Lenders are more hesitant to grant loans to small businesses experiencing financial difficulties. To overcome this potential problem, you can take certain steps to help you company secure loans when it needs them.

- Think about having a line of credit, even if your company does not use it. The only costs are renewal and usage-related fees, but it may be worth the cost to have a loan ready to go when you need it. Furthermore, if your company maintains a certain level of deposits and is considered to be a valuable customer, lenders are frequently willing to waive those fees. Just remember that

lines of credit are a way to finance something for a short period of time, generally less than 12 months. Consider financing some of your operations with loans, even if the amounts are small. This will allow you to build a credit record with lenders.
- Make efforts to anticipate your borrowing needs before they arise and while your company's financial condition is satisfactory. Loan approvals "on-the-fly" and loans to companies with financial problems are not easy to secure.

Create goodwill by referring other businesses to your lenders

If you are happy with your lenders, refer other businesses to them, particularly those that are financially responsible and are likely to repay their loans. This is a good way to develop mutually rewarding relationships. A lender's job is not easy when it comes to finding new businesses. Meeting sales goals directly impacts lenders' compensation and they will be grateful for your gesture. Lenders can also be a good source of referrals, because some of their customers could be your potential customers. My advice is to discontinue referring businesses to lenders or to reduce referrals to a minimum, if your actions become a one-way street and you never see anything in return.

Ask your lending officer whether he or she has the authority to approve your loan

Lending institutions have elaborate loan approval processes. Your lending officer may not be the only person approving your loan request. What does this mean to you? If your lending officer has that authority, then you can learn about his or her expectations and preferences. The next step is to meet those expectations. If necessary, play their personal tunes and stroke their egos to achieve your goal.

If there are other lenders involved in loan approval, you are not likely to meet them in person and plead your case. You should work to build a rapport with your lender to make him or her plead your case. In addition, try to inquire about the preferences of those other individuals and do your best to address them in your Request for Loan Approval. Although this task is a bit more difficult, with proper preparation you can achieve good results.

Unconventional ways of finding prospective lenders
To increase your chances of finding the right lending institution, I recommend meeting prospects at social gatherings, business expos, and other social and professional events. You can kill two birds with one stone using this strategy, finding prospective lenders and future business associates.

I have also heard from some business customers that they use their accountants and lawyers to get in touch with "good" or reputable lenders. An accountant or lawyer will not want to jeopardize his or her relationship with your company by sending you to a lender with a bad reputation. Some small business entrepreneurs have even used pressure tactics to facilitate loan approval. They agree to hire an accounting or law firm, as long as those firms could facilitate or to some extent guarantee loan approval. I personally think that this request is a stretch of what your attorneys and accountants can do, but perhaps it will work for you.

What to do when your lending officer has changed employers and is inviting you to follow him or her
This situation arises more often than you might think. Suppose you really enjoyed the level of service provided by a particular loan officer and would like to stay with him or her. Lenders traditionally jump ship for two reasons. Firstly, their lending institutions have been acquired by other companies, and they are either forced to leave or prefer to work somewhere else. Secondly, they change lending companies in search of more money and better opportunities. It is not an easy decision for a small business owner to move to another lending institution, for several seasons. The key reason: Moving loan, deposit, and other financial services is not easy and interruptions can adversely impact your company. While your lending officer may be the best lender in the world, the new employer may limit his or her ability to offer you the best services and products.

To ensure that you are getting the best deal possible, you should follow these simple steps: 1. Ask your lender if the products and services offered by the new lending company are equal to or better in quality than the ones you currently have; 2. Ask what your lender will do to make your relationship transfer as painless as possible. Can he or she give you any guarantees? No good lender will lie to you and risk losing your respect and your business relationship. Consider whether you are happy with the existing lending institution and whether the departure of your existing lending officer will affect the quality of your business relationship. If not, think twice before you decide to follow your lender. If you are unhappy with the lending company, perhaps this is also the time to shop around and see what your options are. In addition, your existing lender may be willing to lower pricing on your loans or other services, if you let it be known that you are considering taking your business somewhere else. Use the situation as a bargaining chip.

When you are overwhelmed by the process of securing loans

Looking for loans can be a very trying process. It requires good strategy and persistence. If you are overwhelmed, you are not the only one. I hope that with the help of my book you will be able to secure loans or even determine that loans are not right for your business. Obtaining financing is one of most important aspects of running a successful business, and this is not something to cut corners on. Be patient – your goal is to get your foot in the door. Consider working with lenders to be part of your education. If you spend the time to learn how to secure small business loans the very first time you need loan financing, your future attempts will be less stressful and more successful. The more loans you get and repay successfully, the easier it will get.

I would like to wish you luck in searching for loans for your small business, and will be glad to hear your questions and feedback, including suggestions on how I can make this book an even more powerful source of knowledge. Remember that doors do not open to those who do not knock on them. Make your lenders and their loans work hard to make your company prosperous and successful!

You may reach me by email at neil@loanfinancingguide.com.
Also visit www.loanfinancingguide.com.

APPENDICES

APPENDIX 1

Converting your business and personal goals into the language lenders will understand and appreciate

Bridge table: translating my business goals into the terms lenders will understand and appreciate

You	You as lender:" My goal is to approve loans to companies that can repay them."
Bakery owner I want to create a bakery that will be a destination for residents of all local towns to go for their fresh bread and baked goods. I want to train a couple of reliable employees, which will allow me to work only 4 to 5 days a week and still ensure that the quality of my baking goods is superior.	Based on my research, my business will be able to retain 300-400 repeat customers and reach sales of $$$ in the first year of operations. This will allow me to repay your loan within NNN years. I want to manage and control my bakery's cash flow on a daily basis, secure the best possible price from suppliers, and take advantage of all space and equipment resources to produce the highest profit possible. This will allow my business to outlive financially weaker competitors.

Architectural firm owner I would like to create a firm that will be the most reputable interior design company focusing on corporate clients. I would like to hire and retain only the most talented people in the field.	I would like to focus on projects in the $$$-$$$ range that offer good profit margins. This niche is neglected by many larger competitors due its relatively small size. I will also focus on collections to ensure that my company's cash flow is least likely to be interrupted, which will ensure timely debt and interest payments. To afford attracting talented individuals, I would like to pay particular attention to project budgeting and managing the entire design and construction process. This will ensure maximum profitability, prevent financial losses, and ensure timely loan repayment.
Owner of food processing equipment manufacturing company My goal is to improve the quality and design of food processing equipment. My equipment will be equal to or exceed the quality of the equipment offered by my large competitors. My goal is to grow my customer share as rapidly as possible in this lucrative and growing market niche.	My goal is to invest 10% of my company's revenue every year into research and development to continuously improve the equipment we manufacture. My goal is also to invest sufficient amounts of money every year into our facilities. My goal is to retain business of at least 6 new customers every year with a minimum order size of $$$. In addition, my goal is to focus on customer retention. This will ensure sufficient cash flow to make loan payments.

Electrical contractor I am determined to double my company in size in three years and will have a backlog of jobs for at least 8 months at any given point of time. I am determined to retain my customers by high quality service, a workmanship guarantee, and good follow-up service.	I am determined to increase my company's revenue twofold with a goal of having 10% profit before taxes (show a financial plan). Considering the demand for electrical contractors and the fact that even companies with poor quality of work are booked for 1-2 months in advance, my NNN years of experience in NNN types of projects will help ensure my 8-month booking target. I am determined to have a company that stands 100% behind its work, which is outlined in our detailed, written agreements (not typical for competitors). Loyal customers and ample work will translate into satisfactory cash flow to repay your loan.

Software developer for healthcare industry	My company will address NNN needs of hospitals that are only partially satisfied by these competitors: NNN. My small team's expertise revolves around NNN areas, and we are proud of the following successfully-designed software: NNN. Here is our development timeline and here is list of hospitals that have shown the interest in our product.
My company will develop software that will exceed all competing products by the ease of use, ability to manage all stages of inpatient and outpatient process, and ability to be customized to the needs of my customers.	
My company will have every third hospital in New England use my software in five years.	There are NNN hospitals in New England, and my company will begin targeting the ones that are not happy with their existing software. The competitors are charging $$$, and my company will offer our software for $$$ on a trial basis, which will make transition a lucrative proposition. I raised $$$ from equity investors and set aside $$$ to guarantee loan payments until the company reaches profitability in NNN months.

Non-profit job training organization CEO	
I am determined to manage an entrepreneurial non-profit organization, which will earn sufficient money to offer our customers the training and resources traditionally available to for-profit companies. I am determined to offer our employees benefits and compensation that will approach those of the private sector.	I am determined to grow our revenue with more than 70% reliance on product and service income, rather than on government grants. Our past experience shows that this goal is realistic. After paying our staff and making loan payments, all profits will be used to support our social purpose. To attract dedicated and skilled staff, I am determined to care for our employees the same way we care for our customers. Our historical operating profits in excess of 5% provide evidence that we can generate sufficient cash to fund our programs and pay our lenders.

APPENDIX 2

A possible Income Statement format

Revenue or Sales	$100,000
Less: Cost of goods sold	-$20,000
Gross profit	**$80,000**
Less: Operating expenses	-$50,000
Operating profit	**$30,000**
Less: Interest expenses	-$5,000
Plus: Other income / expenses	$2,000
Income before tax	**$27,000**
Less: Tax expense	-$7,000
Net income	**$20,000**

APPENDIX 3

A possible Statement of Cash Flow format

Cash flow from operating activities:	
Receipts	$70,000
Disbursements	-$50,000
Net cash flow from operating activities	**$20,000**
Cash flows from investing activities:	
Purchases of investment securities (e.g. stock)	$0
Capital expenditures (e.g. purchase of equipment)	-$5,000
Net cash flow from investing activities	**-$5,000**
Cash flow from financing activities:	
Repayment of bank loan(s)	-$5,000
Proceeds from bank loan(s)	$20,000
Owners' distributions	-$24,000
Net cash flow from financing activities	**-$9,000**
Net change in cash	$6,000
Cash at the beginning of period	$11,000
Cash at the end of period	**$17,000**

(Arrows from the three net cash flow subtotals point to: **Total**)

APPENDIX 4

Spreads or summary of the applicant's tax returns (income statement and balance sheet)

Historical Income Statement of Restaurant X

Financial Statement type	2000 Tax return		2001 Tax return		2002 Tax return	
Revenue	$673,354	100.00%	$603,412	100.00%	$610,422	100.00%
Cost of sales	$181,000	26.88%	$153,120	25.38%	$150,235	24.90%
Gross profit	**$492,354**	**73.12%**	**$450,292**	**74.62%**	**$460,187**	**75.39%**
Operating expenses						
Officers' salary	$41,150	6.11%	$40,050	6.64%	$38,400	6.29%
Employee salaries & benefits	$170,762	25.36%	$181,491	30.08%	$189,421	31.03%
Rental expenses	$73,490	10.91%	$79,200	13.13%	$84,300	13.81%
Advertising	$5,900	0.88%	$10,211	1.69%	$7,649	1.25%
Depreciation & amortization	$13,305	1.98%	$15,380	2.55%	$14,680	2.40%
Other operating expenses	$109,710	16.29%	$99,544	16.50%	$102,374	16.77%
Total Operating expenses	$414,317	61.53%	$425,876	70.58%	$436,824	71.56%
Operating profit / -loss	**$78,037**	**11.59%**	**$24,416**	**4.05%**	**$23,363**	**3.83%**
Interest expense	$10,840	1.61%	$8,940	1.48%	$9,125	1.49%
Other income / -expense	$0	0.00%	$0	0.00%	$0	0.00%
Income before tax	**$67,197**	**9.98%**	**$15,476**	**2.56%**	**$14,238**	**2.33%**
Taxes	$0	0.00%	$0	0.00%	$0	0.00%
Net Income	**$67,197**	**9.98%**	**$15,476**	**2.56%**	**$14,238**	**2.33%**

Historical Balance Sheet of Restaurant X

ASSETS	2000		2001		2002	
Cash and cash equivalents	$32,450	17.38%	$16,557	10.80%	$8,559	6.37%
Inventory	$12,441	6.66%	$11,500	7.50%	$14,320	10.66%
Other current assets	$0	0.00%	$0	0.00%	$0	0.00%
Total current assets	**$44,891**	**24.04%**	**$28,057**	**18.30%**	**$22,879**	**17.04%**
Gross fixed assets	$78,720	42.15%	$79,720	51.99%	$80,549	59.98%
-Accumulated depreciation	-$22,768	-12.19%	-$31,996	-20.87%	-$40,804	-30.38%
Net fixed assets	$55,952	29.96%	$47,724	31.13%	$39,745	29.59%
Note receivable from principal(s)	$0	0.00%	$0	0.00%	$0	0.00%
Prepaid expenses	$2,500	1.34%	$2,300	1.50%	$3,800	2.83%
Net intangibles	$69,400	37.16%	$63,248	41.25%	$57,376	42.72%
Other assets	$14,000	7.50%	$12,000	7.83%	$10,500	7.82%
Total assets	**$186,743**	**100.00%**	**$153,329**	**100.00%**	**$134,300**	**100.00%**
LIABILITIES and SHAREHOLDERS' EQUITY						
Overdrafts	$0	0.00%	$0	0.00%	$0	0.00%
Accounts payable	$8,656	4.64%	$3,420	2.23%	$3,120	2.32%
Bank note payable	$26,623	14.26%	$19,908	12.98%	$15,462	11.51%
Credit card payable	$6,884	3.69%	$5,745	3.75%	$5,127	3.82%
Current portion of LTD	$15,800	8.46%	$15,800	10.30%	$15,800	11.76%
N/P to officer	$0	0.00%	$0	0.00%	$3,897	2.90%
Other short-term liabilities	$0	0.00%	$0	0.00%	$0	0.00%
Total current liabilities	**$57,963**	**31.04%**	**$44,873**	**29.27%**	**$43,406**	**32.32%**
Long-term debt	$63,200	33.84%	$47,400	30.91%	$31,600	23.53%
Other liabilities	$0	0.00%	$0	0.00%	$0	0.00%
Total liabilities	**$121,163**	**64.88%**	**$92,273**	**60.18%**	**$75,006**	**55.85%**
Shareholders' equity						
Common stock	$41,000	21.96%	$41,000	26.74%	$41,000	30.53%
Retained earnings	$24,580	13.16%	$20,056	13.08%	$18,294	13.62%
Total equity	**$65,580**	**35.12%**	**$61,056**	**39.82%**	**$59,294**	**44.15%**
Total liabilities and shareholders' equity	**$186,743**	**100.00%**	**$153,329**	**100.00%**	**$134,300**	**100.00%**

APPENDIX 5

An approach to estimating your business' ability to make loan payments.

[1] **Operating profit / -loss**	$53,474	-$708	$16,766
[2] + Depreciation / Amortization	$151,600	$198,671	$226,114
[3] - Total capital expenditures	-$180,833	-$219,082	-$243,091
[4] - Cash taxes	-$16,840	-$3,160	-$11,703
[5] - Distributions	$0	$0	$0
[6] - Other adjustments	$0	$0	$0
[7] **Operating cash flow**	$7,401	-$24,279	-$11,914
[8] + Capital expenditures financing	$0	$0	$0
[9] **Operating cash flow after financing**	$7,401	-$24,279	-$11,914
Interest	$3,201	$2,611	$1,950
Current portion of LTD	$0	$0	$0
[10] **Total debt service**	$3,201	$2,611	$1,950

[1] Operating profit or loss is found in your company's income statement. The income statement can be found in your tax returns and in compiled, reviewed, or audited financial statements prepared by your accountant. The operating profit or loss is the net difference between your revenue and operating expenses. Revenue and expenses must be related to your daily business activities and exclude income and expenses unrelated to your day-to-day business (e.g. revenue from sale of business assets, investment income unless your business is an investment firm, interest expenses, income taxes, etc.).

[2] Depreciation and amortization expenses are also listed in the income statement. They are non-cash expenses included in operating expenses. Therefore, lenders add them back to determine your business' operating cash flow.

[3] Total capital expenditures means investments into or purchases of fixed assets, which includes furniture, equipment, building, automobiles, renovations, etc. Your capital expenditures may be reduced by the sale of some of your existing assets. Here is one way to calculate your capital expenditure: Net Fixed Assets of the recent year MINUS Net Fixed Assets of the previous year PLUS Depreciation Expense of the recent year. Some lenders use what they call maintenance capital expenditure. This number is often less than your actual annual capital expenditure. It is the minimum amount necessary to maintain your company's fixed assets in satisfactory condition and maintain current level of revenue. This number is frequently less conservative and many lenders use the actual capital expenditure figure.

[4] Cash taxes are the actual taxes your business paid during a particular year. Businesses may occasionally pay more taxes than posted in the income statement (to offset the next year's taxes) or pay less than is recorded in the income statement (you will most likely have to pay them next year).

[5] Distributions or cash withdrawals by a business owner occur most frequently in businesses where owners report and pay business income taxes in their personal tax returns (e.g. subchapter S corporations or partnerships). As a result, the owners have to withdraw a percentage of the company's net income to pay taxes. However, this is not applicable to sole proprietors, who report taxes on their personal tax returns. They do not take distributions because there are no business tax returns to file and everything flows through personal tax returns.

[6] Other adjustments that increase or decrease the operating cash flow. The extent to which lenders are likely to make adjustments is dictated by his or her organization's credit culture. You should not be concerned with this category. A lender's goal is to smooth out some unusual fluctuations in your business' operating cash flow. For example, when you are planning on buying a building, lenders add back the rent your company paid in the most recent fiscal year, because it is now

considered to be a saving. Another example is a loan taken from the business by its owner. This loan will be typically subtracted from the operating cash flow because it is equated to a distribution.

[7] The operating cash flow (often referred to as OCF) is very important. This is what lenders focus on when evaluating your company's ability to make debt payments. This line shows whether your company produced enough operating cash to pay or service debt. OCF will be compared to proposed (expected or future) annual debt payments to estimate whether your company is able to generate sufficient cash to make those payments.

[8] Capital expenditures financing is a loan or the owner's capital contribution that was used to finance the acquisition of fixed assets. You will typically see loans in this line. The owner's cash contributions are also recorded here, but they are not as frequent as loans. This line item is important as it offsets some of the costs of capital expenditures and makes your operating cash flow higher in the following line.

[9] Operating cash flow after financing takes into account loans or sometimes owner's capital contributions used to help finance capital expenditures. This financing usually increases your operating cash flow and improves your ability to secure loans.

[10] This last line item is pretty straightforward. It contains interest expense and current portion of long term debt (principal due in the next 12 months). If you are borrowing on a line of credit or a similar type of loan that does not require recurring principal payments, you will only have to fill in the interest line. For new debt payments, you may use a conservative, assumed interest rate to estimate interest expense.

CPSIA information can be obtained at www.ICGtesting.com
Printed in the USA
LVOW10s1923250813

349534LV00001B/165/A